double duty

duty second edition

The Parents' Guide to Raising Twins,
from Pregnancy Through the School Years

• • • • • •

Christina Baglivi Tinglof

New York Chicago San Francisco Lisbon London Madrid Mexico City
Milan New Delhi San Juan Seoul Singapore Sydney Toronto

D1059627

Library of Congress Cataloging-in-Publication Data

Tinglof, Christina Baglivi.
    Double duty : the parents' guide to raising twins, from pregnancy through the school years / by Christina Baglivi Tinglof.—2nd ed.
       p.   cm.
    ISBN 13: 978-0-07-161344-6 (alk. paper)
    ISBN 10: 0-07-161344-7 (alk. paper)
    1. Twins.   2. Child rearing.   3. Infants—Care.   4. Pregnancy.   I. Title.

HQ777.35.T56   2009
649'.144—dc22   2008045689

1 2 3 4 5 6 7 8 9 10 11 12 13 14 15 16 17 18 19 20 21 22 23 24   FGR/FGR 0 9

ISBN 978-0-07-161344-6
MHID   0-07-161344-7

Interior design by Mary Lockwood

McGraw-Hill books are available at special quantity discounts to use as premiums and sales promotions or for use in corporate training programs. To contact a representative, please visit the Contact Us pages at www.mhprofessional.com.

This book is printed on acid-free paper.

To my sons, Joseph, Michael, and Matthew; and in loving memory of their grandmother, Rosemarie Marasco Baglivi, who would have spoiled them rotten.

Contents

Acknowledgments   xi

Introduction   xiii

1. So You're Having Twins   1

Just the Stats, Ma'am   1

Why the Increase?   2
*Fertility Drugs • Assisted Reproductive Technology •
Age • Birth Control Pills • Inherited Trait • Women Who
Already Have Had Children • Women Who Already
Have Had Fraternal Twins • Race • Body Type • Diet,
Environment, and Other Factors*

Twin Types   5
Fraternal • Identical • Semi-Identical

Determining Twin Type   7

Myths or Miracles?   8

Now It's Your Turn   9

2. Fifty Pounds and Still Gaining—
Thriving in a Multiple Pregnancy   11

Prenatal Care   12
*Choosing a Doctor • But I Don't Feel High Risk •
Prenatal Tests • Possible Maternal Complications •
Possible Fetal Complications • Preterm Labor •
Interventions to Help Prolong Pregnancy • If Your
Babies Are Born Prematurely*

Pregnancy Lifestyle Changes 31
How We Feel • Getting Plenty of Rest • Exercising Sensibly •
Is It OK to Have Sex? • When to Leave Work • Staying
Comfortable • Traveling • Diet

Tips for Increasing Chances of a Healthy Pregnancy 46

One Final Thought 47

3. It's All in the Planning 49

Nursery Essentials 49
Crib • Bouncer Seats • Car Seats • Strollers • Swing •
Clothing • Blankets • Toys • Diapers • Baby Monitor •
Snugly Sack • Playpen/Port-a-Crib/Pack-n-Play • Don't
Waste Your Money • Future Nursery Items

Two for the Price of One? Money Matters 56
Reevaluate Your Budget • Double-Duty Items •
Breastfeeding • Do It Yourself • Freebies, Coupons, and
Discounts • Secondhand Rose • One More Thing . . .

Getting the Family Ready for Twins 61
The Birth Experience • Select a Pediatrician • Cook Ahead •
S.O.S.—Getting Help • Preparing Older Children •
Taking Care of Business • How Are You Feeling, Honey? •
Choosing Names

It's Almost Time 71

4. The First Month: Dirty Little Secrets
   Parents Won't Tell You 73

Developmental Milestones 73

Keeping Your Head Above Water—First Month
   Survival Tips 74
Keep Notes • Take Care of Yourself • Sleep When You Can •
Don't Answer the Phone • Prioritize Chores • Learn to Tell
Your Twins Apart • Create Baby Stations • Recognize
Postpartum Depression

Feeding Your Babies   79
Breastfeeding • Bottle Feeding • Nighttime Feedings

Bathing and Dressing   92
Of Special Concern—Bathing and Dressing Preemies

The Fussy Hour—Will You Live Through It?   94
Fighting the Fussy Fest

Playtime   95

Bonding with Twins: The Truth Versus the Myths   95
Techniques to Promote Bonding

Four Weeks and Counting   99

5. Months 2 Through 6   101

Developmental Milestones   101

Home Alone   103
*Troubleshooting • Putting Babies on a Schedule • Support
Groups and Play Groups*

Traveling Overnight with the Twins   114
Traveling by Car • Traveling by Plane • Europe and Beyond

Getting Out Without the Twins   118
Finding a Babysitter

Is Three a Crowd? Nurturing Sibling Relationships   120
Tips for Nurturing the Parent-Child Relationship

The Postpartum Body   123

Applause   124

6. Months 7 Through 12   125

Developmental Milestones   125

The Exploring Twins   127
Babyproofing Your Home • Safety on the Go

Treating Twins as Individuals 131
Should You Separate Twins for a Day? • *To Dress Alike or Not to Dress Alike?*

Life After Infancy 138
Keeping the Marriage on Track • *Dad's Changing Role*

Introducing Solid Foods 142
Feeding Your Twins • *Eating on Their Own*

What a Year It's Been! 144

7. The Toddler Years 145

Developmental Milestones 145

As Toddlers Grow—Singing the Naptime Blues 147
From Two Naps to One

Exploring the Twin Bond 149
The Beginning Bond • *Nature Versus Nurture Theory*

Speech Development 153
How Language Begins • *The First Words* • *Speech Difficulties in Twins* • *Is There a Secret Twin Language?* • *Are Your Twins on Target?*

The Terrible Twos—Are They So Terrible? 158
Banding Together for Mischief • *A Question of Discipline* • *Fighting Between Twins* • *Toilet Training*

In Sickness and in Health 164

One More Pair? 165

8. School Days 167

Developmental Milestones 167

The Great Debate: Should You Put Your Twins in the Same Classroom? 168
Advantages of Placing Both in the Same Class • *Advantages of Placing Both in Separate Classes* • *What the Research Tells Us* • *How to Choose What's Best for Your Kids*

Twins and Friends 173
Tips to Encourage Outside Relationships

Twins Asserting Their Independence 176

The Need to Compare and Contrast Twins 177
The Pitfalls of Labeling • Playing Favorites

Twins as Adolescents and Adults 181

The Last Word 182
*This Too Shall Pass • The Grass Is Always Greener on the
Other Side of the Fence • Go with Your Gut*

Appendix 185

*Suggested Reading and Bibliography • Twin Resources and
Websites • National Twins Clubs • Free Samples of Baby
Products and Coupons • DNA Test Kits and DNA Labs*

Index 197

Acknowledgments

Many heartfelt thanks to all those who helped with this second edition. First and foremost to my agent, Betsy Amster, and my editors, past and present—Sarah Pelz and Fiona Sarne—whose continued support is greatly appreciated. And to the dozens of parents who took time from their busy lives to thoughtfully answer questions about life with young twins. Their insightful and personal anecdotes add depth and substance to this text.

I'm truly grateful to Donna Fairholm, Nicole from Australia, Melissa Dunlop Skinner, the Teschow/Ormerod family, Roxanna, Sheri Weese, Jenean Working, Robin Gray, Kathleen Lomax, Melinda Ott, Heather Richelson-Hopkins, Stephanie Faulkner, Pamela Damico, Bill and Marci Peebles, Alden Perkins, Amy Maddux, Vickie Skidmore, Jennifer Corey Ferguson, Brenda Carle, Jill Bachman, Julie Sech-Biondolillo, Shari Meltzer, Shawna Burns Singh, Analisa, Kim Clayton, Corey Petrie, Anne-Marie Hunt, Joanne Arrandale, Jennifer Krasusky, Laura Leafstrand, Tami Turner, Marlene A. Prenez, Jackie Crockett, Sarah Wheeler, Amanda Armitage, Jyll Petro, Jennifer Hallman, Deb Lynch, Amanda Stanger, and Jesse Armitage (the Dad).

And finally, to my family—thanks to Kevin and my boys for pitching in and working as a team so I could have time to write!

Introduction

When I wrote the first edition of *Double Duty* more than 10 years ago, my fraternal twin sons were two-year-old toddlers. In those days, just as I would sit down with an intriguing research paper ready to pound away on the keyboard explaining the latest study on twins, they'd decide it was time to run in opposite directions.

That was then, and what a decade it has been since.

My little toddlers have grown to teenagers. They still take off in opposite directions, but this time it's usually on skateboards. Ten years ago, my boys also greeted a new baby brother, and I got to find out what it's like to mother a singleton (yes, it is different than parenting multiples). Those of you with single-born children know that I am wise to mention him here, as singletons sometimes get overlooked when there are twins in the mix. Many, including my younger son, don't take kindly to that fact!

It's been a good decade for new parents expecting twins, too, as we've learned so much more about how to increase the chances of a healthy twin pregnancy (load up on those calories and protein) and how multiples develop cognitively, physically, and emotionally (no, they won't suffer if you place them in the same kindergarten class).

Learning the News

Like most of you reading this book right now, my husband, Kevin, and I learned about the impending arrival of our double bundle of joy while in the ultrasound room. Just six weeks into my pregnancy, I lay on the examining table, craning my neck to see the video screen, with Kevin by my side. (A high level of human chorionic gonadotropin [hCG] in my blood prompted the early visit and subsequent diagnosis.) Barely visible to our untrained eyes, two tiny hearts blinked in unison against a dark backdrop, flickering like interstellar fireflies. My doctor's suspicions were confirmed—we were expecting twins.

Our first reactions were similar to the ones you probably felt when you learned the news: disbelief, excitement, and, of course, fear. Like you, I was worried about the pregnancy and whether our babies would be born healthy. I had read that twins often show up prematurely (three weeks on average) and that it was extremely important that I take exceptional care of myself to ensure a happy outcome. My efforts paid off—I carried my sons to term (they induced me at Week 39). Joseph weighed about 6 pounds, 8 ounces; Michael was 6 pounds, 12 ounces. Yet part of it was sheer luck as I never knew the importance of weight gain for moms carrying multiples. (Thankfully I indulged my constant craving for big, juicy hamburgers—I would pick one up while on the way home from work at least twice a week!)

Like you, too, we hit the bookstores to find a pregnancy book on multiple births. In those days, not many filled the shelves. These days, however, it seems that books on multiple births are bountiful, but you, dear reader, just happened to find the right one.

Welcome to the Second Edition of *Double Duty*

Throughout the second edition of *Double Duty*, you'll find plenty of new material, beginning in Chapter 1, So You're Having Twins, where you'll discover all sorts of fun twin facts. Did you know, for instance, that the days of double-digit increases in twinning may finally be coming to an end as the medical community calls for single embryo transfer (SET) instead of the two, three, or more embryos that were standard practice for in vitro fertilization (IVF) just a few years ago? You can also feel confident as a new parent of twins when you guess your twins' zygosity (the medical term for twin type) as studies have shown that merely following a simple checklist results in 95 percent accuracy.

Diet is stressed in Chapter 2, Fifty Pounds and Still Gaining—Thriving in a Multiple Pregnancy, as recent published reports show that not only the more weight a mom-to-be with multiples gains results in a longer gestation and heavier babies, but when she puts it on (the earlier the better) is just as important. The chapter also delves further into twin-to-twin transfusion syndrome, a rare but sometimes devastating disease that affects 15 percent of identical twin pregnancies who share a common placenta (most monozygotic or identical fetuses have two placentas). But recent research offers lots of hope as new diagnostic and surgical breakthroughs emerge in the medical community every day.

Not only does the latest, cutting-edge research play a big role in this edition of *Double Duty*, but parents have a stronger voice as well. From the United States, Canada, and Australia, 39 families with young twins volunteered to answer a lengthy survey covering not only their prenatal and postnatal experiences but the more practical aspects of life with infant twins, such as what baby equipment they couldn't live without (turn to Chapter 3, It's All in the Planning, to find out) and what they thought was a waste of time (can anyone say Diaper Genie?). In Chapter 4, The First Month: Dirty Little Secrets Parents Won't Tell You, parents share their clever tricks for handling nighttime feedings whether you'll be bottle feeding or breastfeeding your infants. And their responses surrounding feeling the "baby blues" and their postpartum bodies were touchingly honest and insightful, sure to offer you both comfort as well as inspiration.

Once the chaos of the first month subsides, Chapter 5, Months 2 Through 6, focuses on troubleshooting, with advice on how one person can handle stressful situations alone, like when your twins cry at once. Chapter 6, Months 7 Through 12, takes a look at twins' developing autonomy, with parents offering unique ways of carving out "alone time" with all their children. (Wouldn't you love to have had the mom who lets each of her kids play hooky from school for a special mother-and-child day?) We even dig up that old debate of whether dressing twins alike affects twins' quest for individuality. I'll tell you what the research says—it's not what most parents believe.

Yet *Double Duty* still includes the old favorites such as Top Five Lists, quick references to the most popular ways of handling your duo from the Top Five Birthday Party No-Nos to the Top Five Twin Gadgets, as well as Developmental Milestones—many unique to twins—so that you know what to expect both physically and emotionally from your doppelgängers in the coming months. For instance, don't expect your babies to start actively interacting until well after they've reached their first birthday. But once they've hit that marker, their "twinness" will blossom and become fascinating to observe. Twins will temporarily choose roles in their relationship—one will become the leader, the other, the follower. But several months later, they often reverse positions (just to keep you on your toes).

This new edition includes Chapter 7, The Toddler Years, where parents lament about the "naptime blues." Just when you thought you had this twin thing down, the little critters remind you that toddler twins often band together to cause all kinds of mischief, especially at naptime. And you'll never laugh as hard as when you read the "terrible two tales," as parents regale you with stories of double naughtiness. Not to worry—these seasoned moms and dads are on top of it and have plenty of advice to help you circumvent it all. Finally, Chapter 8, School Days, closes out the book with the latest on the hotly debated classroom placement issue. While recent research shows that some twins benefit from being placed together, there are no studies to show that it harms twins' self-esteem and sense of autonomy.

Even though there's plenty of new information in this second edition, one thing has remained constant—*Double Duty* still shares strategies about the day-to-day circumstances that new parents of twins face, from how to nurse or bottle feed two babies at once to getting twins on the same schedule. Whether you're concerned about giving each baby enough individualized attention or deciding whether to put them in the same class in school, *Double Duty* has the answer. Let it be your guide to life with multiples. Happy trails!

•1•

So You're Having Twins

Parents of twins hear all sorts of odd questions and misinformed comments about twinning from friends and family (and even strangers), such as "Are they *paternal* twins?" and "I thought all same-sex twins were identical!" High school science class covered the basics, but most folks have forgotten why and how this phenomenon happens. What follows in the next few pages is a crash course in Biology 101 so that you may go out and reeducate the world on the miracle of twinning. Now, class, pay attention. . . .

Just the Stats, Ma'am

A staggering 95 percent of all multiples are twins, and more than 125 million sets roam the world today. The number of multiples, particularly twins, has been on the rise since the early 1980s, when doctors first learned how to make women superovulate, or release multiple eggs in one cycle. In 2005 (the most recent year for which statistics are available), the United States reported more than 133,122 live twin births, compared with approximately 110,670 in 1998 (the year *Double Duty* was first published). Yet the number of twins was only 68,339 in 1980. That's a 70 percent jump in 25 years. To bring those numbers a bit more in focus—during the 1980s, twins occurred in one in every 80 to 90 live births; in the late 1990s, it was one in every 40 to 45 live births. Today, twinning happens in about one in every 33 live births.

And what about other countries? Has twinning been on the rise around the world as well? You betcha! Canadian twin births, for instance, have also spiked through the years, rising more than 30 percent from 1974 to 1990. In the Netherlands, twinning has soared nearly 65 percent from 1970 to 1995. Australia, England, France, Denmark, Brazil, South Korea, Japan, and many other countries have also seen their share of double strollers these days.

Why the Increase?

The explosion of twinning is due to a number of complex biological, medical, and environmental factors. Some are well known and well documented; others are just speculative at best (but fun to read about nonetheless).

Fertility Drugs

During the late 1970s, fertility drugs became widely available to couples who had problems conceiving due to ovulation disorders. Clomiphene citrate (Clomid), the most common of all ovulating-inducing drugs, stimulates a woman's hypothalamus and pituitary glands to pump out more hormones, which in turn fuel the ovaries to produce and release more eggs at the time of ovulation. A woman who takes clomiphene citrate increases her chances of twinning by 10 percent. (Although some doctors say the percentage is much higher—especially if a woman already ovulates on her own.) A woman's likelihood of a multiple birth rises even further if she takes more potent, injectable fertility drugs such as human menopausal gonadotropin (Perganol), human chorionic gonadotropin (Pregnyl), or follicle-stimulating hormone (Fertinex).

Assisted Reproductive Technology

In vitro fertilization (IVF), the most common of all assisted reproductive technology (ART), has been helping infertile couples conceive for more than 25 years now. It involves removing eggs from the mother (following a round of ovulating-inducing drugs), fertilizing them in the laboratory using her partner's sperm, and then implanting the embryos back into her uterus. Several are implanted at once to increase the likelihood of success. In recent years, however, the procedure has become so success-ful that two, three, or more embryos are often viable, contributing to the explosion in multiples births. (One report published in the journal *Twin Research* back in 2003 noted 40 percent of IVF babies results in twin-ning.) To help stem this tide, many in the medical community are call-ing for single embryo transfer (SET), especially for women under the age of 35 who have a longer time frame for conceiving. It may be work-ing, too, as the year-over percentage increase in twinning is not nearly as dramatic as it has been in the past and is finally leveling off.

One mom who was interviewed for this book got pregnant with twins through IVF after having only two embryos implanted. She was shocked since just a few years earlier she conceived a singleton, a son, after transferring a whopping 10 embryos and "hoping for a miracle."

AGE

A woman who delays childbearing until after age 30 is also at a greater risk of twinning. As a woman gets older, she produces higher levels of gonadotropins (peaking between ages 35 and 39), hormones that stimu-late the ovaries to release more eggs. Two of these hormones are the follicle-stimulating hormone (FSH) and luteinizing hormone (LH), both responsible for ovulation. A 35- to 40-year-old woman is three to four times more likely to have twins than a woman who is 20 to 24 years old. Older moms have clearly had an impact on the rise in twinning. In fact, more twins were born to moms aged 45 to 49 in 1997 than dur-ing the entire decade of the 1980s.

BIRTH CONTROL PILLS

A woman who gets pregnant shortly after the cessation of certain types of birth control pills has a greater chance of conceiving twins as well, although the results have been found to be inconclusive in some stud-ies. (Of the 39 moms interviewed for this book, one mom of identical boys conceived almost immediately after stopping birth control pills. Coincidence? Perhaps.)

INHERITED TRAIT

Yes, twins do run in families, but only fraternal twins (not identical) and only through the female bloodline. Some women inherit a gene for hyperovulation, or the predisposition to produce multiple eggs in a single cycle. So if your mom is a fraternal twin, or has a set in her family, that could explain why you are expecting twins.

Women Who Already Have Had Children

Due to hormonal changes, the more children a woman has, the more likely she will conceive twins with each successive birth.

Women Who Already Have Had Fraternal Twins

Indeed, lightning can strike the same place twice. A woman who has already given birth to fraternal twins without the use of fertility drugs doubles her chances of repeating it again with her next pregnancy since she's already proven that she's fecund, or able to produce abundant offspring!

Race

African races (especially West Africans) have the highest incidence of twinning (they are about 20 percent more likely than Caucasian women to have twins), followed by Europeans, and then Mexicans. Asian women have the lowest incidence.

Body Type

If a woman is tall and heavy with a body mass index (BMI) of 30 or above, her chances of having fraternal twins is significantly greater than a woman with a BMI of 20 or less since overweight women tend to produce more FSH.

Diet, Environment, and Other Factors

If you search hard enough, you can find a host of other theories that explain the rise in twinning. *The Journal of Reproductive Medicine*, for instance, reported in 2006 that women who regularly eat dairy products are five times more likely to conceive fraternal twins than women who don't. Researcher and author of the study, Dr. Gary Steinman, theorized that the synthetic growth hormones given to some diary cows could be the culprit. Once the insulin-like growth hormone enters a woman's bloodstream through her high diary consumption, it accelerates ovulation. And bingo—fraternal twins!

Large amounts of folic acid have also been associated with twinning. Even yams, rich in the compound phytoestrogens and a dietary staple in many parts of Africa, are thought to promote hyperovulation. And finally, there's even a report or two proclaiming that an abundance of daylight induces hyperovulation. That could explain the higher number of multiples born in early spring in some Nordic countries as they benefit from nearly 12 hours of sunlight during the summer solstice.

Twin Types

There are two definitive types of twins—dizygotic (DZ) or fraternal, who share 50 percent of their genes (at best), and monozygotic (MZ) or identical, who share 100 percent. There's growing speculation surrounding a third type called semi-identical or half-identical twins, as well. Fertilization determines twin type.

FRATERNAL

The most common type of twins, fraternal, occurs when two separate eggs are fertilized by two separate sperm. Fraternal twins have different DNA (at most they share only 50 percent) and often don't look anything alike. They're simply womb-mates; two siblings sharing the same space for nine months. Since so many different factors are associated with dizygotic (or fraternal) twinning, their frequency varies from country to country anywhere from 4.5 percent to 6 percent.

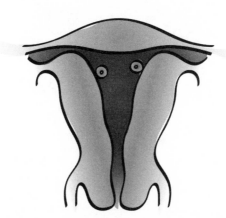

Fraternal twins are formed when two eggs are fertilized by two sperm.

Identical

A mysterious anomaly in nature, identical twins occur when one egg, fertilized by one sperm, splits into two embryos. The mystery doesn't end there. Depending on when the zygote splits determines how the embryos will grow in the womb. If the zygote splits within the first three days of fertilization, it's a diamniotic-dichorionic pregnancy, each baby having his or her own placenta and amniotic sac. If, however, the zygote splits between Days 3 and 9, each baby will have his or her own sac (diamniotic) but share one placenta (monochorionic). If it splits between Days 9 and 12, the result will be monochorionic and monoamniotic—one sac and one placenta. And finally, if the mass splits after Day 12, the result will be conjoined twins.

Identical twins share the exact same DNA and, therefore, are always the same sex (except in a few extremely rare cases). They often look exactly alike (but surprisingly have different fingerprints). Identical twins account for only 30 percent of twinship and unlike fraternal (or dizygotic) twins, their prevalence worldwide remains fairly constant at 0.3 to 0.4 percent. It's interesting to note, too, that although the incidence of identical twins is random in nature, science does inadvertently help it along. According to research studies, women who undergo IVF have a two to three times higher chance of having identical twins. The reason why is still unknown.

Twenty-five percent of identicals are mirror twins—that is, many traits like dental patterns, hair swirls, and birthmarks appear on oppo-

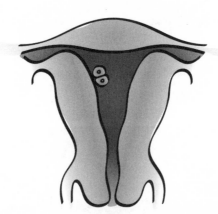

Identical twins are formed when one egg fertilized by one sperm splits into two embryos.

site sides of each twin's face. Many mirror twins are opposite handed, too. One twin is a lefty, while the other is a righty.

Semi-Identical

The theory goes that if an egg splits first and is then fertilized by two separate sperm, semi-identical (or half-identical) twins are the result. Since they receive the same exact genes from their mother but different genes from their father, these twins share about 75 percent of each other's DNA, not the 100 percent of identical twins nor the 50 percent shared by fraternal twins. For years the validity of this third twin type has been questioned, but a 2007 study published in *Human Genetics* verified that it does in fact exist (however rare). So the next time you see "fraternal" twins that look remarkably like "identical" (how about actresses Mary-Kate and Ashley Olsen?), think semi-identical.

Determining Twin Type

Unless your twins are a boy and a girl, determining twin type can be tricky, especially immediately following their birth. (Don't all newborns look alike?) As the twins get older, varying physical appearance or growing similarities will shed some light as to their type, yet many fraternal twins look remarkably alike. The only reliable method to determine twin type is DNA testing or blood testing of the umbilical cord. In the past both procedures were too costly, keeping many parents wondering, but in recent years more and more home DNA kits offer an easier (and cheaper) way of learning your twins' true zygosity through cheek swabbing and hair samples. For a couple of hundred dollars and a few weeks of wait time, parents can definitively get their answer. (Refer to the Appendix for a list of labs that provide kits and perform DNA testing.) Still, several recent research studies all conclude that a parent's best guess (by way of a twin similarity questionnaire) as to zygosity is about 95 percent accurate.

It seems that mother does know best.

We had a lot of ultrasounds and the doctor always told us the boys were fraternal, but then we had the level two ultrasound and they told us that there was a possibility that they could be identical. We are not really 100 percent on whether they are identical. Now as they are older they have some more distinct features that make them look different, but I do sometimes confuse them myself if I only see one at a time. I have mixed feelings about the whole thing. I'm not really sure, but I'd lean more toward fraternal.

Myths or Miracles?

Think you've got this biology stuff figured out? Let's find out! Answer true or false to the following twin tales.

Twins occur every other generation.

False. Just an old wives' tale. Twinning can happen in any generation. It just seems to skip with some families since hyperovulation is strictly a female phenomenon. A mother can pass this hereditary trait on to her twin son who obviously doesn't ovulate but who can pass it on to his daughter who then can someday give birth to twins, and presto, the myth continues.

Most twins don't look alike.

True. Only one-third of all twins are identical. Fraternal twins are simply siblings who share a common birthday.

If there's only one placenta, the twins must be identical.

False. This isn't necessarily so. Sometimes two separate placentas fuse together, giving the appearance of one. The only true way to tell if twins are fraternal or identical (unless they are boy and girl) is through testing.

If you're an identical twin, your chances of having twins will increase dramatically.

False. Identical twins are nature's toss of the dice and aren't passed down from family to family. Only fraternal twins run in families. So if you're an identical twin, your chances of having twins aren't greater than anyone else's.

Now It's Your Turn

As science continues to look into the fascinating world of twinning and why some women are more susceptible to it than others, you're bound to be a bit too busy changing diapers and doing extra laundry to notice. In the meantime, however, you're now armed with the latest twin facts and figures so you can go out into the world and dispel the myths! As a newly chosen "multiple missionary," it's your turn to educate the world (or at least your family and friends) about twinning.

•2•

Fifty Pounds and Still Gaining— Thriving in a Multiple Pregnancy

When I went in for a routine visit at 16 weeks, I was sporting a decent bump at that point. But my first child was big, so I didn't think much of it. The doctor took a look at my tummy and said, "You're looking a little big." She got out the stethoscope and listened a few minutes. Then she left the room in search of an ultrasound machine. On her way out the door she asked, "Do twins run in your family?" I thought she was kidding, but sure enough, a few minutes later we were looking at two babies on the screen. The first thought that went through my head? Minivan.

Forget the old saying, "You're eating for two." You're eating for three—a sometimes awesome task. And while most women can expect to gain 25 to 30 pounds with a singleton pregnancy, the American College of Obstetricians and Gynecologists recommends gaining at least 35 to 45 pounds if a woman is carrying twins. In fact, research shows that the more weight a woman expecting twins gains—especially during the first two trimesters of her pregnancy—the less likely she'll run the risk of a premature birth.

Twin pregnancies at any age are considered high risk, a term that often sounds worse than it is. Remember, most mothers-to-be breeze through a twin pregnancy without a complaint. Unfortunately, others are confined to bed rest early on due to complications stemming from an engineering glitch in the human body—women were designed to carry only one fetus at a time. But there's plenty that you can do to help ease your anxieties about your pregnancy—educate yourself on multiple births, increase your protein and calorie intake significantly (more on that later in this chapter), take frequent rests, and follow the advice of your physician (but always ask questions if you don't agree). This chapter focuses on your pregnancy and what you can do to help bring healthy babies into the world.

Prenatal Care

You dream that the birth of your children will be a day of joy with few, if any, complications. Yet you can't ignore that little voice in the back of your head that keeps whispering, "What if there's a problem?" While no one can guarantee smooth sailing, good prenatal care provides the best chance for a healthy outcome for both you and your babies. Keep all scheduled doctor's appointments. And to get the most out of your visits, keep a written list of questions that you want to remember to ask your doctor. With so much information exchanged during a typical prenatal exam, you should think about taking a small tape recorder with you, too, so you can review your doctor's advice later when you have a chance to take it all in.

CHOOSING A DOCTOR

Your relationship with your obstetrician is an important one. Since you'll be asking him or her many questions throughout your pregnancy and deciding on a host of important issues, including which prenatal tests to undergo, you should feel a strong sense of trust and comfort. To find a qualified obstetrician, call your local hospital's doctor referral service, ask other moms of twins in your area, or contact your local Mothers of Twins Club for a list of recommendations.

Try to choose a health care provider with experience in multiple births and high-risk pregnancies. You and your doctor should have similar views on pregnancy and birthing as well. Does he or she routinely perform cesarean sections on all multiple births, while you feel strongly about trying to have a vaginal birth? What treatment does he or she prescribe if problems do arise? Many tests and techniques involving a multiple birth vary widely, and a few are considered controversial. Do you agree with your physician's point of view? If not, you might want to interview another obstetrician.

You might want to also consider signing on with a perinatologist, or maternal-fetal medicine (MFM) specialist, an obstetrician who specializes in high-risk pregnancies. You can use a perinatologist as either your primary-care physician or as a consultant (think of this doctor as a second pair of eyes trained to spot potential problems or complications associated with a multiple pregnancy).

I think if I were to do anything differently, I would have stayed with the high-risk OB/GYN instead of my regular OB. Maybe the high-risk doctor would have caught the problem that caused my preterm labor. I would have also pushed to see my doctor after our last ultrasound when the technician said one baby was head down. I delivered four days later. (Ashlyn and Taylor, fraternal girls, were delivered at Week 28. Ashlyn weighed 2 pounds, 1 ounce while Taylor came in at 2 pounds, 7 ounces.)

Hospital Affiliation

Even if you take excellent care of yourself and follow your doctor's advice to the letter, twins sometimes show up early (three weeks on average), and in some cases very early, requiring an extended stay in a neonatal intensive care unit (NICU). Neonatal intensive care units are ranked as follows: Level I is a basic care unit for uncomplicated births; Level II (specialty) cares for infants who come into the world with moderate problems such as apnea but are expected to recover quickly; and Level III (subspecialty) focuses on comprehensive care for extremely high-risk newborns such as those born in critical condition.

When searching for your obstetrician, try to find one affiliated with a Level III hospital with a top-notch NICU. Otherwise, if your newborns do need to be placed in the NICU and your hospital doesn't have one, your babies will be transported to a better-equipped facility, away from you.

Chances are that your twins won't need the NICU. Of the 39 surveys completed for this book, 12 sets of twins spent some time in the NICU. Two of those sets required only a day, and one pair stayed two days (enough time for their moms to recover from the rigors of childbirth). But one set of fraternal girls stayed for 10 long weeks. The median time (excluding the highest and lowest scores) for all, however, was only 10 days.

My girls were in the NICU for 10 days. The hardest part was
being transferred to my room and hearing all the mothers and
their babies and knowing mine wouldn't be coming. I cried a lot.
But looking back, I was given the opportunity to recover before I
took on the daunting task of more than one. I visited every chance
I got, even after I was released. Somehow knowing they had each
other when I wasn't there gave me some feeling of peace.

BUT I DON'T FEEL HIGH RISK

Even if you feel great throughout your pregnancy, multiple births are more likely to run into medical complications than singleton deliveries and, therefore, earn the term *high risk*. For this reason, moms carrying twins are monitored more closely than those carrying singletons. You'll visit your doctor more often—usually once a month for the first trimester, every two weeks during your second trimester, and then weekly during your final trimester.

PRENATAL TESTS

In addition to more doctor visits, you'll also undergo more prenatal tests. Even healthy twin pregnancies require more poking and prodding than singleton pregnancies. However, some doctors prescribe more tests than others. Following is a brief list of standard tests that you'll encounter. Each has its benefits as well as its risks and should be discussed at length with your obstetrician.

Ultrasound

What? One of the most widely used prenatal tests, ultrasound (or sonogram) uses high-frequency sound waves and takes only a few minutes to perform. It's relatively painless and one of the least invasive prenatal procedures. The doctor or technician rubs a thin layer of lubricating jelly across a pregnant woman's lower abdomen and then moves a transducer across the area. As the sound waves bounce off the babies, an image appears on a television screen. (If you're in the very early stages of pregnancy, however, your doctor may perform a transvaginal ultrasound instead during which a lubricated probe is gently inserted into the vagina. This type of scan is even more accurate than a traditional ultrasound as the device can come into closer contact with the fetal sac.)

Why? Ultrasound is extremely important for a mom expecting twins. Not only can it confirm a multiple pregnancy, but it accurately predicts the babies' due dates and gestational age. It's also used to identify intrauterine growth restriction (IUGR) in which one or both fetuses' weights rank in the less than 10 percent range for gestational age. For those moms expecting identical twins, ultrasound can determine the number of chorions (outer membranes or placentas) and amnions (inner membranes or amniotic sacs), which is helpful in diagnosing the presence of twin-to-twin transfusion syndrome (TTTS). Ultrasound can also recognize possible maternal problems such as placenta previa as well as fetal malformations such as spina bifida, Down syndrome, or abnormalities of the brain, heart, liver, or kidneys. Later in pregnancy it's used to show the position of the babies to determine the best mode of delivery and to monitor fetal growth and weight. It also measures cervical length (a strong predictor of preterm labor especially prior to Week 30) and the amount of amniotic fluid surrounding the babies. Ultrasound can determine the sex of the fetuses, though not with complete reliability.

When and How Often? For women expecting multiples, an ultrasound is routinely given about Week 7 to confirm a multiple pregnancy. It's performed again near Week 18 to check the structure of the placenta and to detect any fetal abnormalities. Following Week 24, ultrasounds are given every few weeks to ensure the babies' continued growth and to monitor for possible complications.

Pros and Cons. Considered a safe procedure since no harmful x-rays are involved, ultrasound is one of the least invasive prenatal procedures. Parents' concerns about the health of their babies are immediately put at ease without lengthy waits for lab results. The benefits in safely accessing the fetuses in a multiple pregnancy make ultrasound a commonly recommended test.

Amniocentesis

What? Amniocentesis, generally considered a safe procedure, involves removing a small amount of amniotic fluid from the amniotic sac, the bag of liquid that surrounds the fetus (or fetuses). The genetic material found in the fluid is then studied in a laboratory. With the help of ultrasound, a safe insertion spot away from the fetus is established and then a needle is inserted through the abdominal wall and into the uterus. The procedure takes about 30 minutes to perform, and the patient may feel a small amount of discomfort. A mom-to-be carrying twins may have two amniocenteses performed—one for each amniotic sac.

Why? Amniocentesis is used most often to detect chromosomal abnormalities such as Down syndrome in fetuses of women older than age 35 (age 33 if the mom-to-be is expecting multiples). The test can also recognize autosomal recessive diseases like sickle-cell anemia, cystic fibrosis, and Tay-Sachs disease. It can confirm the baby's sex and, therefore, is important for a family with a history of sex-linked diseases such as hemophilia. During the third trimester, amniocentesis is invaluable in determining the maturity of a baby's lungs if premature delivery seems inevitable.

When and How Often? Although amniocentesis is usually performed once between Weeks 16 and 20, the clinician may order a second toward the end of the pregnancy to establish the maturity of a baby's lungs when a woman is experiencing problems in her pregnancy and premature delivery is unavoidable.

Pros and Cons. Waiting the required week or two for amniocentesis results can put a strain on any couple, but the peace of mind that follows after hearing that the test results are negative helps families relax and enjoy the remaining months of pregnancy. On the other hand, a major downfall to amniocentesis is the relatively late time in the pregnancy it is performed, making it difficult for those waiting for genetic analysis and who may be facing the decision of whether to abort. Furthermore, amniocentesis is more difficult to perform on a twin pregnancy since both sacs must be evaluated and on occasion the second sac can't be located; it's very expensive (about $1,500 for each test, usually covered by insurance); and there's a small chance of spontaneous abortion (less than 0.06 percent, but 2.7 percent in women with multiples) or infection.

Chorionic Villus Sampling

What? Chorionic villus sampling (CVS) is relatively new in the medical community. With the aid of ultrasound, a catheter (thin tube) is inserted into a woman's cervix (transcervical) or a thin needle is inserted through her abdomen (transabdominal) and a small amount of the developing placenta cells are extracted and then cultured in a laboratory. There's very little discomfort to the patient who undergoes transcervical CVS, the feeling is similar to a pap smear; transabdominal CVS patients may find the pinch of the needle slightly more uncomfortable.

Why? The test can detect chromosomal abnormalities such as Down syndrome, cystic fibrosis, and Tay-Sachs disease, among others.

When and How Often? Chorionic villus sampling is usually performed once between Weeks 10 and 12.

Pros and Cons. Since CVS can be performed early in pregnancy, some couples choose it instead of amniocentesis. Primary results are available within 48 hours (compared to the standard two weeks for amniocentesis results). There's a lower complication rate—both physically and psychologically—if selective termination is chosen when one fetus has an abnormal result. The downside of CVS, though, is its slightly higher risk of spontaneous abortion (approximately 1 percent for singleton pregnancies; about 4 percent for multiple pregnancies) as well as the possibility of fetal limb defects (documented in patients who had the procedure done prior to 10 weeks). There's also a chance of amniotic leakage. In addition, the test can't detect neural tube defects such as spina bifida.

Maternal Serum Alpha-Fetoprotein

What? Maternal serum alpha-fetoprotein (MSAFP) is a painless blood test used to measure a specific protein made by the baby (or babies) and circulated in the mother's bloodstream.

Why? The test offers a noninvasive way to analyze the health of the fetus. High levels of alpha-fetoprotein (AFP) can indicate a neural tube defect such as spina bifida, or it can simply mean a multiple pregnancy. Low levels may indicate Down syndrome.

When and How Often? The test is usually given once between Weeks 16 and 20.

Pros and Cons. Considered by some to be a controversial test, MSAFP's biggest drawback is its sometimes inaccurate results in the form of false positives and false negatives. Women with false positive results require additional tests, worrying them needlessly. If levels of AFP are low, an expensive amniocentesis may be prescribed to confirm or deny the existence of Down syndrome. If levels are high, parents might jump to the wrong conclusion that their baby has a neural tube defect, only to discover later through ultrasound that the blood results simply mean that the couple is expecting twins. This blood test is not necessary for women who already plan on having an amniocentesis.

> *I received a call from the doctor's office stating that the alpha-fetoprotein numbers were abnormal. They told me I needed to head straight in for an emergency sonogram. Terror is an accurate word for what was going through my mind. My husband and I went together to the office, and I told him I was fully prepared for the worst. When the technician started the sonogram, she said, "Well, there's your answer. You have twins!" My husband and I cried. We were so relieved.*

Nonstress Test

What? For a nonstress test (NST), external ultrasound monitors are attached to a woman's abdomen in order to monitor the fetal heartbeat, fetal movement, and possible uterine activity. The results are printed out and then evaluated by a physician.

Why? The test is usually used during the third trimester to assess fetal well-being due to stress from maternal high blood pressure, overcrowding in the uterus due to multiples, or other medical problems associated with a high-risk pregnancy.

When and How Often? When deemed necessary by a physician, a NST is administered weekly during the last trimester, usually after Week 30, and sometimes twice weekly after Week 32 (approximately Week 28 for women expecting identical twins).

Pros and Cons. This is a painless and safe procedure. There are no immediate drawbacks, except that it can take up to an hour to perform.

Possible Maternal Complications

The following are complications that may happen during pregnancy, but chances are they won't happen. Statistically, mothers carrying twins do experience more problems, but keep in mind that statistics are only as reliable as the population they study. Since most research is carried out at major medical centers, many participants are already deemed high risk. The odds are that if you take good care of yourself by eating right (increase those calories and protein!), getting enough rest (put those feet up!), heeding the "warning signs," and visiting your doctor regularly, your babies will be born big and healthy. **But be proactive and always call your doctor if you experience any unusual symptoms.**

Bleeding

Spotting is common in early pregnancy and seems more serious than it usually is. In fact, of the moms I interviewed, four experienced bleeding in the early weeks, prompting a visit to their doctors and the ultimate discovery of their twin pregnancies. One mom spotted at Week 14 but carried her babies all the way to Week 38!

While the causes of spotting are not always clear (some women bleed on and off throughout their entire pregnancies without any ill effects to their babies), a woman experiencing vaginal bleeding should err on the side of caution and notify her physician. In some cases, bleeding in the early months could mean an impending miscarriage of one or both babies, an ectopic pregnancy, or an incompetent cervix in which the cervix prematurely dilates (if caught early enough the cervix can be sutured closed and later opened nearer to delivery). In late pregnancy, bleeding may mean that the placenta is separating from the uterus (placental abruption) or partially covering the cervix (placenta previa), both require immediate medical attention. Bleeding during sexual intercourse may indicate a cervical polyp or vaginal infection.

Edema

During pregnancy, the amount of fluid increases in your body. As the babies grow and crowd the pelvis, circulation slows, causing a swelling of the ankles and hands. Standing for long periods of time exacerbates the situation. When this happens, it's best to lie down with your feet propped up. Wearing support hose that's not too tight at the waist can also counter the effects of mild edema. However, if your hands continue to swell and your face becomes swollen, it could be a sign of toxemia and should be reported to the doctor immediately.

Preeclampsia

Preeclampsia, or toxemia, is characterized by extremely high blood pressure. The cause is not known, but it affects about 5 percent of all pregnancies, and nearly 20 percent of twin pregnancies. Careful screening of blood pressure, monitoring swelling of the hands and feet, and testing for protein in the urine, especially during the third trimester, are the best ways to assess whether a woman is at risk for developing preeclampsia. Other signs include headaches, blurred vision, rapid weight gain (a pound or more in a day), and abdominal pain. In recent years, with improved screening and the use of magnesium sulfate as a routine treatment, the incidence of preeclampsia is lower. Still, if it goes unchecked and untreated, it can develop into eclampsia, a dangerous condition for both mothers and babies.

Gestational Diabetes

Gestational diabetes develops during the latter half of the second trimester or early part of the third trimester and then can resolve itself after the babies are born. The condition occurs when there is a change in a pregnant woman's glucose metabolism as her body puts more demands on the pancreas to produce more insulin, resulting in insulin resistance. If a woman develops gestational diabetes, her chances of preeclampsia increase. She may also experience complications during delivery and might be at risk for developing adult-onset diabetes later in life. A glucose tolerance test is given during the second or third trimester to screen for the disease. Women with borderline gestational diabetes are put on a strict diet high in protein and low in carbohydrates, while women who develop the condition require insulin during the remainder of their pregnancies. Unfortunately, women expecting multiples increase their chances of developing gestational diabetes. (Seven moms interviewed developed the condition. All were able to keep their insulin levels under control, and five delivered past Week 34.)

Anemia

Anemia occurs when a woman's body isn't producing enough red blood cells to transport oxygen to her babies. As the babies grow, they deplete the mother's iron supply. In severe cases, anemia can cause preterm labor. A diet rich in iron and folic acid may not be enough to prevent anemia, and often a doctor will prescribe additional iron supplements—especially if a woman develops a mild dilutional anemia after 28 weeks of pregnancy, as most do.

Placenta Previa and Abruptio Placenta

A condition where the placenta covers part of or the entire cervix, placenta previa is twice as likely to happen to a mother expecting twins as a woman carrying a singleton. Usually, the only symptom of this condition is slight bleeding without any discomfort. After the mother's and babies' conditions have been assessed through ultrasound, bed rest is usually recommended. If placenta previa occurs during the early months of pregnancy, the placenta often grows up and away from the cervix, but if it occurs later in pregnancy, and the condition does not correct itself, then cesarean delivery is required.

Abruptio placenta (placental abruption), on the other hand, is when the placenta begins to peel away from the uterine wall, usually during the third trimester. Symptoms include vaginal bleeding and abdominal pain, sometimes quite severe. If the abruption is mild, the doctor may admit the mom-to-be to the hospital for observation. If the babies are in distress, however, the doctor may choose to deliver them immediately by cesarean.

Cesarean Delivery

Nearly 50 percent of twins are delivered by cesarean, due in large part to added complications associated with a multiple delivery and to a medical community that shies away from breech (baby in feet-first position) or transverse (baby in horizontal position) deliveries. In about half of all twin pregnancies, both infants will be in the vertex (head-down) position—but in the remaining 50 percent, one or both babies are either in the breech or transverse position. Sometimes after the first baby is born vaginally, the physician can manually massage the mother's abdomen to turn the second baby into the head-down position, thereby avoiding a cesarean delivery.

To many moms, the thought of delivering their babies under the harsh lights of an operating room is scary, especially to those who have never spent a day in the hospital. You can ease your anxiety by understanding the procedure and knowing what to expect and when.

The procedure itself is quite quick—only about 30 minutes. Post-op—suturing the uterus and abdomen and monitoring your vital signs—takes a bit longer, about an hour or two. After your abdomen has been shaved and cleaned with an antibacterial solution, a catheter is inserted into your bladder to keep it empty during surgery, and an IV is inserted, usually on the back of your hand, to administer both fluids and regional anesthesia (either a spinal or epidural so you can be fully awake but not feel anything below your waist). A curtain is raised just below your chest so both you and your husband or birthing partner (who's seated right next to your head) won't have to watch the procedure. Next, a transverse (horizontal) incision is made just above the bikini line. The doctors then remove both babies and placentas, and carefully stitch up the uterus as well as the abdomen. Although you won't feel any pain, you'll feel a slight tugging during the whole operation.

Usually both babies will be cleaned and weighed right there in the operating room (my husband even had the opportunity to cut their umbilical cords there as well), and you'll get a chance to finally say hello to your bundles for the first time. Immediately following the operation, you'll be sent to a post-op room where a nurse will watch your vital signs while your babies will be sent temporarily to the nursery for evaluation. You'll meet up again either in the post-op room or in your hospital room (some moms choose to have their babies stay in the nursery a while longer so they can get a bit of sleep following surgery).

Once the anesthesia wears off, many moms require additional medication to help ease the discomfort from the surgery. Once your doctor gives the OK, getting out of bed and walking the halls (I pushed both bassinets up and down the corridors twice a day while in the hospital—they acted as a makeshift walker) helps promote the healing process, making recovery time much faster. Stitches are usually removed in seven days; you won't be able to do any heavy lifting or driving for several weeks.

POSSIBLE FETAL COMPLICATIONS

Once again, it's important to remember that most babies do just fine. Not too long ago, babies born at a little more than 2 pounds had a slim chance of survival; these days they have an 85 percent survival rate, and new records are being broken all the time. The following fetal complications are listed merely to keep you informed.

Twin-to-Twin Transfusion Syndrome

Twin-to-twin transfusion syndrome (TTTS) is a rare but serious, progressive disorder that occurs in about 15 percent of monozygotic monochorionic twins, identical twins who share a common placenta. Identical twins with two placentas (dichorionic) and fraternal twins are not at risk of developing this condition. The earlier the onset of TTTS, the greater the risk of infant mortality. The cause is due to an abnormal vascular connection within their shared placenta—an uneven amount of blood flows between the two twins so that one receives too much blood while the other doesn't receive enough. The disease is characterized by a fetal weight difference of more than 20 percent and a large discrepancy of amniotic fluid between the fetuses' dividing membranes. Both babies suffer—the donor is often born underweight and anemic, while the recipient can experience jaundice, respiratory problems, or even heart failure.

Medical intervention has been successful. One method, amnioreduction, in which the excess fluid is removed from the recipient's sac, shows promise. But critics point out that while it decreases the risk of a premature birth, the underlying cause of the disease continues. As the fluid returns to the recipient's sac, several procedures may be necessary. For severe cases of TTTS, a recent Australian research study found that the use of laser therapy to correct the connecting blood vessel resulted in a significantly higher survival rate than amnioreduction.

For a mom with a monozygotic pregnancy, it's important to identify and determine chorionicity early so that she can be closely monitored by her doctor to watch for any signs of TTTS.

If a family finds themselves with a TTTS diagnosis, knowledge is power. There are many wonderful resources offering information as well as support for parents expecting twins with TTTS, including the Twin-to-Twin Transfusion Syndrome Foundation (tttsfoundation.org) and the TTTS message board available through the *Twins* magazine website (twinsmagazine.com). Two families from the surveys I collected experienced TTTS. Both sets of now three-year-old male twins are doing just fine!

> *My pregnancy was complicated with TTTS. I had five*
> *amnioreductions to manage the fluid, and I was on bed rest for two*
> *months. I was monitored very closely. At 29 weeks I had an*
> *accidental septostomy (a hole was created in the membrane*

*dividing the boys). Ultrasound then showed the membrane had
actually been shredded and there was no longer anything
separating the babies. From that point it was treated as a
monoamniotic pregnancy. A different treatment could have brought
a very different outcome, especially since Matthew had 70 percent
of the placenta and Isaac only 30, which may not have been
enough to sustain him if we had had laser surgery. (Matthew and
Isaac were born at 32 weeks and weighed 4 pounds, 4 ounces and 3
pounds, 3 ounces. They required a month-long stay in the NICU.)*

Intrauterine Growth Restriction (IUGR)

Intrauterine growth restriction (sometimes referred to as low birth weight, or LBW) happens in about 15 percent of twin pregnancies when one or both fetuses are growing poorly and weigh below the 10th percentile for gestational age. The fetuses may not get enough nutrition due to maternal, fetal, or placental problems. Maternal smoking, alcohol and narcotic use, high blood pressure (preeclampsia), genetics, poor nutrition, and twin-to-twin transfusion syndrome are all contributing factors. While IUGR can occur in fraternal twins, it's more common in identical twins (even those without TTTS) where one fetus gets a larger share of the placenta mass. Studies show that an early and proper diagnosis confirmed by ultrasound is paramount to a healthy outcome.

*There was a decent weight difference between the girls and that was
identified early on but it wasn't TTTS. There was a weight
discrepancy from the first ultrasound at Week 16 but always just a
little bit under [the 20 percent] where the doctors get nervous. At
Week 33, the ultrasound showed an even bigger weight discrepancy,
but the doctor redid the measurements a few times and got it closer.
After delivery, they theorized that it was a cord placement issue
that caused the weight difference. They're a little closer in weight
now, but the bigger twin at birth continues to be the bigger twin
now. (Kate and Sarah, identical girls, were delivered at Week 38
and weighed 5 pounds, 11 ounces and 8 pounds, 3 ounces.)*

PRETERM LABOR

The number one problem of moms expecting twins, preterm labor happens when a pregnant mom goes into labor prior to Week 37 of gestation. Nearly 50 percent of mothers carrying twins experience preterm labor. The cause is not clear, but it's speculated that poor weight gain through inadequate nutrition (so eat up!), an infection in the mother, a history of prior preterm labor, preeclampsia, smoking, maternal age (under age 16 or older than 35), benign uterine tumors, or simply overcrowding in the uterus due to multiple fetuses could contribute to preterm labor. In some cases, preterm labor can be stopped through drug therapy. Since it's widely known that the cervical length decreases during the third trimester of a multiple pregnancy, which is a precursor to preterm labor, several studies recommend getting regular transvaginal ultrasounds starting the second trimester to measure cervical length for women who are at risk of developing preterm labor.

Seventeen out of 39 moms completing my survey went into preterm labor (before Week 37) and subsequently delivered early. Nine of those 17 missed Week 37 by just a few days, and their babies spent little or no time in the NICU. The mean, or average, week of delivery for the entire group of 39 moms was Week 36 and 2 days; the mode, or most common week of delivery, however, was Week 38. Even though one woman delivered at Week 35 and 4 days, her fraternal boys weighed in at 6 pounds each!

> *I felt incredibly "wrong." Something was not right, but I couldn't really accurately describe it. I had my husband take me to the doctor's despite everyone assuring me that it was Braxton-Hicks contractions. It didn't feel like contractions though; it felt like the entire section of my lower back was in a huge back spasm. My head felt like lead, and I was having trouble keeping my mind and eyes focused. (Although this mom was in full-blown labor, doctors were able to stop it, and she delivered at Week 36.)*

Preterm Warning Signs

Labor can come on quickly, and some symptoms can be hard to quantify. One mom told me that she simply couldn't sleep one night and knew something must be wrong. It was; she was in labor.

If you experience **any** of the following symptoms, don't hesitate to call your doctor immediately.

- The onset of contractions (five or more per hour, lasting 40 seconds or longer), not to be confused with normal Braxton-Hicks contractions (lasting 20 to 30 seconds; usually irregular; and disappearing after an hour, a change of position, or drinking lots of fluids)

- Low, dull backache, menstrual-like cramps, or extreme pelvic pressure (as if the babies are pushing down)

- Release of amniotic fluid or mucus plug, a change in mucus appearance, or vaginal bleeding

- Diarrhea, strong intestinal discomfort, or vomiting

- The strong feeling that something is wrong

INTERVENTIONS TO HELP PROLONG PREGNANCY

Some of the complications women experience during a multiple pregnancy can be alleviated with proper and timely medical intervention. You can help prolong your pregnancy by managing risk factors such as diabetes or high blood pressure, loading up on calories and protein in your diet, limiting your stress level (maybe it's time to take a leave of absence from that high-powered job), avoiding fatigue by getting plenty (and I mean plenty) of rest, and taking care of your dental health since gum disease is associated with preterm labor.

Bed Rest

Some doctors still routinely prescribe several weeks of bed rest to prevent premature delivery during a woman's last trimester if she is expecting twins. The most common (and one of the most controversial) medical intervention, bed rest can mean anything from round-the-clock confinement to just a few hours a day, in a semireclining position or lying down completely. With bed rest, some physicians reason, the weight and stress of carrying more than one fetus are taken off the cervix. In addition, they say, more nutrients will reach the babies through the placenta because the mother's blood flow increases.

But bed rest has its critics since there has been no large-scale double-blind research study indicating that bed rest prevents premature delivery (although another study found that while hospital bed rest didn't prevent preterm labor, it did help increase fetal birth weight). Furthermore, critics note, complete bed rest will increase a woman's chances of a blood clot and may actually increase her blood pressure, which often leads to preterm labor. The monotony of bed rest can also cause added stress, and a woman who is inactive frequently eats less and ultimately could harm her babies even more. Still, the benefits of resting in a reclined position are important for any pregnant woman as it reduces stress, rejuvenates mind and body, and helps lessen edema. A good compromise, therefore, is to rest often with your feet elevated—30-minute naps three times a day throughout pregnancy.

> *I rested daily—usually for an hour at work—either in the sick room, out in my car, wherever I could find a place to lie down. I'm sure this made a difference. I also always kept my feet up a lot. I got plenty of funny looks during meetings, but I thought, Too bad, I'm having twins. I'm totally swollen, and I'm putting my feet up. Deal with it! (This mom's tenacity paid off—she delivered her boys Week 37 and they weighed 6 pounds, 1 ounce and 7 pounds even.)*

Drug Intervention

These days, doctors have an arsenal of medication to help slow or stop the onset of labor. Some women who experience preterm labor will be hospitalized and treated aggressively with a magnesium sulfate IV and an injection of a steroid to help the babies' lungs mature more quickly and prevent respiratory problems after birth. Once labor has ceased for more than 12 hours, the expectant mother may be allowed to go home but must continue with drug therapy. Science is working hard at solving the problem, too. In 2007 there was a promising study done in Canada that suggests the topical use of nitroglycerin (yes, the heart medication!) helped reduce preterm labor. Authors of the study believe that it increases blood circulation in the placenta and relaxes the uterine muscles. But they caution that much more research needs to be done before it can be put into clinical use.

> *My girls were in the NICU for seven long weeks. To cope with the stress, I focused all my attention on them, trying to stay informed of their situation. I tried to learn everything I could about the machines they were on—what the machines were doing for them. You just have to take it day by day. Some days we would rejoice in a milestone they accomplished, like getting off of a tube or a machine, or gaining a few ounces. Other days we would cry and*

TOP FIVE WAYS TO KEEP SANE
DURING BED REST

Whether for placenta previa or preterm labor, some women are put on bed rest. It doesn't have to feel like a life sentence, though. Bed rest can be a time to catch up on reading or cuddling older children, who often get lost in the shuffle after twins arrive. Here are some ideas to help make the best of a trying situation.

1. **Rainy-day projects.** Whether it's organizing old photos, knitting a few baby blankets, or catching up on correspondence, we all have household assignments just waiting for the right time to be completed. Now's your chance. Make a list and then complete one a week.

2. **Movie madness.** Take an informal poll from family and friends of their favorite movies, give the list to your spouse, pop some popcorn, and then lie back and relax. Now if you could only find the remote!

3. **The write stuff.** Keep a pregnancy journal noting the personality differences of the two baby boxers duking it out in your belly and how you're feeling from day to day.

4. **Mild exercise.** If your obstetrician gives the OK, contact a physical therapist through your local hospital for a list of simple exercises that you can perform while in bed. Prolonged inactivity is detrimental to your body (as well as your mind).

5. **Parenting Twins 101.** Save the romance novels for your next vacation and instead stock up on books educating you on the joys (and headaches) of parenting twins. Or hit the computer and check out the online pregnancy message boards at *Twins* magazine (twinsmagazine.com).

worry because of a setback. I encourage moms and dads to just be there every day, even if it's just for a few minutes. Look at your babies, take in every tiny inch of them and try to see the beauty of what you've created. Sitting at home later in that empty nursery those visions you've stored in your head will help you get by. Be strong and courageous for your children. My way of coping was to provide as much breast milk for them as possible. I focused my attention on pumping every few hours, and getting to see them every time I delivered the milk to the NICU. That really helped me.

IF YOUR BABIES ARE BORN PREMATURELY

Sometimes even if you've been on top of it throughout your pregnancy and following your doctor's advice to the letter, your babies may decide to show up early. A baby is considered premature when he or she is born prior to Week 37. (Fortunately, though, twins mature in the womb a bit faster than singletons—it's a little bonus courtesy of Mother Nature.) Even if your duo does arrive early, depending upon their weight and health, they may or may not need the care of the NICU. Premature infants are at a much higher risk for low birth weight, defined as infants weighing less than 5 pounds, 8 ounces at term (2,500 grams), and may be more susceptible to a variety of respiratory problems such as apnea (when baby stops breathing for more than 15 seconds and must be revived) and respiratory distress syndrome (RDS, when baby's lungs lack a chemical called surfactant). Some premature babies are more prone to dehydration and have problems regulating their body temperature.

Most premature and low birth weight babies will spend some time in the NICU. (According to my surveys, however, 13 babies who weighed less than 5 pounds, 8 ounces at birth never spent a minute in the NICU. Two sets of these twins actually came in at less than 5 pounds each! They were born little but healthy.) Once there, the babies are placed in incubators (sometimes twins can co-bed in the NICU), given oxygen and intravenous fluids, and usually attached to several monitoring devices. The length of their stay depends on their weight and gestational age as well as any complications that may arise.

Highly trained neonatologists and neonurses tend to their pint-sized patients with great precision and compassion, yet when parents see their babies hooked up to the numerous tubes and high-tech equipment, it can be unsettling. Their babies' appearances don't match that of their prenatal fantasy of rosy-cheeked infants. Disappointment and guilt often set in as parents question their actions of the last months. What went wrong? While understanding that there is nothing that an expectant mother or father could have done to intervene with nature, talking through their feelings with family members, friends, or the NICU staff can help tremendously and allow parents to come to terms with this highly emotional situation.

I had them so early and felt that I had lost out on the pregnancy that I had always imagined. I had missed out on my perfect pregnancy. No one ever thinks that they'll deliver at Week 28. I cried a lot and finally told myself that there was nothing I could have done differently to make it go longer and it was meant to end for some unknown reason to me. The only thing I would have done differently was to talk to my loved ones and let them know how I was feeling and not try to keep it bottled up until I was alone. I was trying to put up a strong front to settle everyone else's concerns for the babies.

TOP FIVE WAYS TO BOND WITH PREMATURE INFANTS

When preemies are confined to incubators, it's often difficult for parents to begin bonding with their children. But there are ways for parents to feel close to their infants even while the little ones are temporarily in the NICU.

1. **Visit often.** Although recovering from childbirth (cesareans especially) is draining, try to visit your newborns at least once a day. Both you and your babies will benefit greatly. Talk to them softly or read to them. Ask if you can leave behind a tape recorder of you singing to them.

2. **Nurse your babies.** Yes, it is possible to nurse even premature infants. Speak with the NICU staff concerning feeding schedules. For extremely early arrivals who often have trouble sucking, you may have to express your milk and nurse your twins via feeding tubes. (For more information, read La Leche's *Breastfeeding Your Premature Infant* or other books available on the subject.)

3. **Experience the magic of touch.** When babies are able, practice "kangaroo care" by holding your seminaked baby (he or she wears only a diaper so you won't get wet) against your bare chest. Drape a blanket over the two (or three) of you to create an intimate cocoon. Research shows that it helps to regulate baby's temperature, heartbeat, and breathing patterns. The skin-to-skin contact can also encourage breastfeeding as baby can smell your milk. Even if you can't hold your babies though, your touch and gentle words will begin the parent-child attachment.

4. **Be inquisitive.** By asking questions about their care and the machines they're attached to and their importance as well as informing yourself about the needs of premature infants, you will ease your fears. Take an active part in your babies' recovery by assisting in their feeding and bathing.

5. **Use a picture to say a thousand words.** Place a photograph of your family inside babies' bassinets along with an article of clothing that you've worn. Your babies will be comforted and begin to associate your scent with you.

Pregnancy Lifestyle Changes

You may not be able to control when your babies decide to show up, but you do have power over your pregnancy lifestyle for the next nine months. From what kind of food you put into your body to how often you lie down and rest, you're in charge. Changing your day-to-day routine for the better will have a positive effect on your pregnancy. Learn to listen to your body and act according to its needs.

Top Five Comfortable Sleeping Tips for Extremely Pregnant Women

By the third trimester, most women find it impossible to get a good night's sleep—I know I did—but with a little ingenuity, expectant moms can get some rest. Start by trying these tips.

1. **Try maternity pillows.** These specially made pillows come in all shapes, styles, and sizes and are used to give back support or belly support. Experiment with various positions and styles until you find the right one.

2. **Place pillows strategically.** If you're on a limited budget, try using the pillows you have at home. A pillow wedged in the corner of your back (have your partner position it just so), one between your knees, and one under your stomach give you all the support you'll need. Just don't move too much in the middle of the night or you'll have to adjust them all over again!

3. **Avoid lying on your back.** While it may be comfortable for some, sleeping on your back can decrease the blood flow to the babies. It will often make you feel lightheaded and, therefore, is not recommended.

4. **Sleep semireclined.** Create a minithrone of sorts on your bed using lots of pillows. Then sleep semireclined with your head resting on a pillow against the wall or headboard.

5. **Experiment with other types of furniture.** I slept on a soft leather couch during my last month (other moms told me they slept on their living-room couches, too). The cushions molded to my body, and the couch back gave me support. Another expectant mom successfully slept for weeks on her living-room recliner.

How We Feel

Everything is magnified for women expecting multiples. With the increased hormones that multiple fetuses produce, morning sickness may be heightened. Expect mood swings and moments of irritability. With the extra weight comes pressure on the stomach causing heartburn (a big complaint from the moms I interviewed), pressure on the lungs (causing breathlessness with every step you take), pressure on the intestinal tract (causing constipation and hemorrhoids), and pressure on the back. Beginning in the middle of the second trimester, expect a degree of pelvic pressure every time you stand. Are you getting the picture? Carrying multiples is a tough job. But just wait, the real work begins once they're born!

Getting Plenty of Rest

Slow down—women carrying twins hear this often from their obstetricians. It can be a major adjustment for women who are accustomed to living life on the go. But as the babies grow and you continue to gain weight, you'll tire more easily and require more rest. Don't fight it —give into it. Try to arrange for several naps during the day where you can fully recline, preferably on your left side (keeping weight off your lungs and helping organs function better). If you continue to work full-time and napping isn't feasible, try to sit in a semireclined position with your feet elevated for at least 20 minutes several times a day.

Exercising Sensibly

I stopped working out almost immediately. Being an older mom I knew the risks, and I didn't want to push it. I would walk but gave up the elliptical machine and weights. I started eating well-balanced meals. I forced myself to cover all the food groups because I worried about the babies getting the nutrients they needed. I probably would have been that way with one but with two, I was uber watchful. (Jack and Luke arrived at Week 35½, each weighing 6 pounds.)

TOP FIVE EXERCISES FOR EXTREMELY PREGNANT WOMEN

Your doctor has just told you to stop all aerobic exercising. Now what? You still have three months to go before the babies come! There are plenty of exercises that even a very pregnant woman can do without increasing her chances for preterm labor. Start by trying these stretches. (Note: Consult your physician first before undertaking any exercise program.)

1. **Tailor's sit.** Sit on the floor, legs crossed, arms at side. Straighten your back as you inhale slowly; then exhale and relax your spine. Repeat 10 times. Next, do 10 Kegel exercises by contracting the pelvic floor muscles, tightening as if you were stopping the flow of urine.

2. **Spinal curl.** Get down on the floor on all fours, keeping your back straight. As you inhale, slowly round your back, lifting your stomach toward the ceiling and rolling your head toward the floor. Then slowly straighten your back, lifting your head as you exhale. Repeat 15 times.

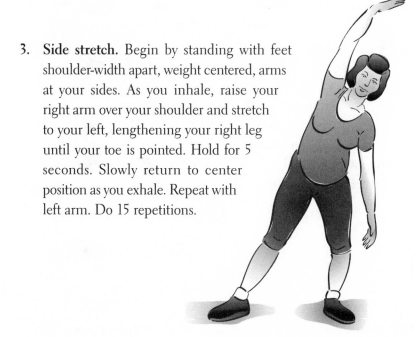

3. **Side stretch.** Begin by standing with feet shoulder-width apart, weight centered, arms at your sides. As you inhale, raise your right arm over your shoulder and stretch to your left, lengthening your right leg until your toe is pointed. Hold for 5 seconds. Slowly return to center position as you exhale. Repeat with left arm. Do 15 repetitions.

4. **Wall push-up and calf stretch.** Stand 1 foot from a wall with your hands in front of your shoulders. Bend your elbows and lean forward, touching the wall and making sure to keep your heels firmly on the floor. Slowly push back, letting your arms do all the work. Do 20 repetitions.

5. **Back and hip stretch.** With your left hand lightly touching the top of a chair, bring your right knee to the side of your belly by placing your right hand under your lower thigh. As you raise the knee, bend your left knee slightly and slowly round your back and head. Hold for five seconds as you feel your back stretching. Release slowly and repeat five times. Switch sides and repeat.

Although exercising helps maintain good circulation and muscle tone, many doctors recommend restricting all aerobic activities at approximately Week 20. For some women, vigorous exercise brings on early labor. Yoga, stretching, walking, swimming, and other forms of moderate activity are usually acceptable for most women expecting twins unless they experience contractions—when it is advisable to stop.

Is It OK to Have Sex?

Sexual desire changes as a woman's body changes. As pregnancy progresses, some women have increased sex drives; others feel so fatigued and nauseated that sex is the last thing on their minds. It's not unusual for husbands to feel less amorous toward their wives as well. Often a frank discussion will reveal their fears of hurting the babies. Yet sex during pregnancy can be a great time for togetherness, a way for husbands and wives to connect emotionally. With no need for contraception, lovemaking can be spontaneous. For many, the stress of trying to conceive has been eliminated, enhancing their lovemaking even further. Don't worry about your size, just approach your lovemaking with a sense of humor (not to mention a sense of adventure, since you'll need to be inventive with your lovemaking positions).

To the disappointment of many couples, though, some doctors recommend abstaining from sex during the last trimester since the female orgasm can sometimes increase uterine activity, prompting preterm labor. In addition, semen contains prostaglandin, which can stimulate vaginal contractions. Be sure to discuss your concerns about sexual activity with your doctor.

When to Leave Work

My obstetrician recommended that I stop work at 24 weeks, which I thought was way too early since I had worked full-time until 36 weeks with my first child. Believe me, by Week 24, I was ready to stop working and stay home.

Doctors' opinions vary regarding the best time for a woman carrying twins to cease working. For some mothers-to-be, leaving work around Week 20, as many doctors suggest, will be a welcome treat, while others face a financial hardship if even a day is missed. Planning ahead by working out a pregnancy budget and making saving money a top priority will help ease the postpartum financial burden.

There are other options to explore as well, such as cutting back on days or hours at work, telecommuting from home one or two days a week, or taking advantage of the Family and Medical Leave Act (FMLA) where eligible employees can take up to 12 weeks of unpaid leave for the birth and care of an infant. If your doctor does recommend leaving work before you had initially planned or orders you on bed rest, be sure to check with your benefits counselor at work to see whether you qualify for disability insurance.

Staying Comfortable

A woman carrying twins in Week 30 is carrying the same weight as a woman carrying a singleton at term. For the mom carrying multiples, comfort becomes harder and harder to achieve. Try the following devices to help ease your aches.

- **Flats or sandals.** During pregnancy it's not uncommon for feet to increase a full size (and often they don't return to their prepregnancy size after birth). To keep your feet comfortable, wear comfy flat shoes, sandals, or a strong pair of flip-flops. But be careful—pregnant woman are not known for their sense of balance.

- **Support hose.** It's not just for the senior set anymore. Wearing support hose will help alleviate swelling of the feet and ankles (edema) and aid in the prevention of varicose veins.

- **Belly support.** Toward the end of the second trimester and throughout the third, the weight of twins on a pregnant woman's back can be intense and painful. Relieve the pressure by wearing a belly support, a minigirdle that wraps around the lower stomach and back. It is available at most maternity stores, through maternity catalogs, and, of course, online.

- **Maternity/nursing bra.** A good maternity bra with flaps that open to enable breastfeeding not only gives support to heavy breasts, decreasing the chances for a backache, but it may also help prevent stretch marks.

- **Maternity pillow.** Essential to a good night's sleep, a maternity pillow should top every pregnant woman's shopping list.

Traveling

Usually, the journey itself isn't harmful to your babies, but with the added chance of preterm labor or other complications that women carrying multiples sometimes experience, most doctors suggest that their patients stay close to home after they reach Week 30.

Diet

Low birth weight (less than 5 pounds, 8 ounces at term) and premature delivery are the two serious complications facing moms expecting twins. Yet expectant mothers who have a proper diet end up with babies who weigh more overall. And since the birth weight of twins is an important indicator in predicting their future mental and physical health, it's extremely important for you to eat well. A visit to a nutritionist who specializes in high-risk pregnancies can help mothers-to-be with poor eating habits streamline their diets. The first priority of any mom expecting twins should be sound nutrition.

> *I was vigilant about eating a lot and eating often. I kept a journal of what I had eaten so that I could make sure my eating was well balanced. For example, when it was time for a snack, I would look to see what I had eaten that day. If, say, I was low on dairy, then I would have some cheese. At the end of the day my goal was to have eaten plenty of protein, dairy, fruits, vegetables, and carbs. (This mom delivered at Week 38, and her twins weighed 5 pounds 4 ounces and 6 pounds 7 ounces.)*

How to Help Avoid Low Birth Weight Through a Proper Diet

Eat up! That's right, you heard me! After reading page after page of what's out of your control during these next nine months, diet is finally the one aspect where you have total control. You can greatly improve your chances of delivering plump, healthy babies just by what and how much you eat. And there's plenty of research these days to back the claim. Reports show that a maternal weight gain of 40 to 45 pounds results in twins averaging 5 pounds 8 ounces (2,500 grams) each. Furthermore, the timing of that weight gain is important, too. Gaining the majority of the pounds early in pregnancy—41 pounds by Week 28—has the strongest impact on babies' weight at birth. Researchers believe that higher weight gain earlier in pregnancy aids in the development and function of the placenta.

For most women, packing it on during the first half of pregnancy will come as a treat since they find themselves in a constant state of hunger. (I found myself stopping for a hamburger often while driving home from work at four o'clock!) Once again, it's Mother Nature's way of stockpiling all those extra calories and fat to use for your babies in the weeks ahead.

How Much Do You Need to Eat?

While a mother expecting a singleton should consume about 2,300 calories and 80 grams of protein a day, a woman carrying twins needs between 3,000 and 3,500 calories and at least 130 grams of protein (one twin researcher advocates 170 grams of protein a day). You can use a

Monday		
Name of Food	Calorie Count	Grams of Protein
Breakfast		
Snack (Mid Morning)		
Lunch		
Snack (Mid Afternoon)		
Dinner		
Snack (Mid Evening)		
Snack (Midnight)		
Total Protein		
Total Calories		

chart like the one provided to track your intake. While it may seem like an incredible goal to reach, the extra calories and protein required are easily met with just a little more than an additional quart of milk a day!

> *I didn't realize until later in my pregnancy how important it was to gain extra weight with twins. I got that information from Internet research, not from my doctor. I only gained 30 pounds, but I only got to Week 31!*

Types of Food Needed for a Healthy Pregnancy

The following are merely diet highlights. Consult your physician or nutritionist about dietary recommendations.

FOODS HIGH IN PROTEIN

(amounts of protein per serving are averages)

Beef, chicken, liver, pork, turkey	4 oz.:	21 grams
Salmon, trout, shrimp	4 oz.:	22 grams
Canned tuna	4 oz.:	28 grams
Cheddar cheese	1 oz.:	7 grams
Cottage cheese	4 oz.:	19 grams
Eggs	1 egg:	6 grams
Whole milk	8 oz.:	8 grams
Powdered milk	1 cup (dry):	25 grams
Yogurt	1 cup:	8 grams
Peanuts	4 oz.:	30 grams
Peanut butter	⅓ cup:	25 grams
Chickpeas (garbanzo beans)	3½ oz.:	20 grams
Lima beans	1 cup:	13 grams
Brown rice	7 oz.:	14 grams
Oats	3 oz.:	12 grams
Spaghetti	5 oz.:	12 grams
Broccoli	1 cup:	5 grams
Spinach (cooked)	1 cup:	5 grams
Corn (cooked)	1 cup:	5 grams

Protein. The amino acids found in protein are essential in building cells and vital in the growth and development of fetal heart, brain, tissue, and muscle. Lack of adequate protein during pregnancy appears to be strongly connected to low birth weight. Clinical studies found that when a mother consumed 80 grams or more of protein per day, her baby would weigh at least 6 pounds at birth. Conversely, when a woman ate less than 45 grams of protein daily, her baby had a 47 percent chance of weighing less than 5.5 pounds. With every additional 10 grams of protein (up to 100 grams per day), the baby's weight would increase by one-half pound at birth. (These statistics are for a singleton pregnancy.)

Meat, fish, dairy, nuts, and legumes offer the best sources of complete protein. Choose sources with a high ratio of protein to fat—in other words, eat broiled fish and skinless chicken instead of fatty or fried meat. Strict vegetarians who abstain from meat products should combine protein sources like legumes with whole grains and nuts to obtain complete protein. A protein-rich diet for the vegetarian should also include an abundance of soy products (soy milk, soy yogurt, and tofu).

Iron. During pregnancy your need for iron increases dramatically. Iron is essential in building hemoglobin (red blood cells), which transports oxygen in the blood. Toward the end of pregnancy, a baby's need for iron rises significantly; and if a pregnant mom doesn't maintain a sufficient level, she will develop anemia, a condition that may lead to pregnancy complications. Iron is also important for a baby's nutrition immediately following birth, and, therefore, it's important to build up a supply prior to birth. In addition, it's important to remember that premature babies are often born anemic—another reason to stock up while you can.

Eating iron-rich foods along with foods high in vitamin C will aid in the absorption of the mineral, raising its efficiency in the body. Most women will find it difficult to meet their daily iron requirement through

FOODS HIGH IN IRON

(amounts of iron per serving are averages)

Beef . . . . 3 oz.: 2 mg

Chickpeas (garbanzo beans)
and other legumes (beans and peas) . . . . 1 cup: 4 mg

Clams . . . . 3 oz.: 10 mg

Dried fruit . . . . 10 to 12: 5.5 mg

Raisins . . . . ½ cup: 2.7 mg

Pumpkin seeds . . . . ¼ cup: 3 mg

Soy products (tofu, miso) . . . . 1 cup: 26 mg

Spinach (cooked) . . . . 1 cup: 4 mg

Wheat germ and other whole grains . . . . ½ cup: 3.3 mg

Other foods high in iron:
Sardines
Sea vegetables (seaweed)
Artichokes

diet alone, so often a physician will suggest taking iron supplements. Take the supplement between meals with a glass of fruit juice or water (avoid taking it with milk) to aid in its absorption.

Calcium. If the thought of drinking four glasses of milk a day doesn't turn you on, consider other sources of calcium like cheese, yogurt, almonds, sardines, tuna, salmon, and a variety of green leafy vegetables. Extra calcium is needed in a pregnant woman's diet to aid in the development of fetal bones, teeth, heart, and nerves and to assist in blood clotting. In addition, some studies indicate that extra calcium reduces the risk of preeclampsia. To aid in its absorption, avoid eating calcium-rich foods with caffeine or fibrous foods such as whole-grain products.

Folic Acid. Folic acid, a B vitamin, is not only needed for baby's growth and development and liver efficiency, but well-documented studies indicate that a diet deficient in folic acid may contribute to birth defects (such as cleft palate and spina bifida, a condition in which the spinal column doesn't close completely) and low birth weight. Raw green vegetables (parsley, cilantro, chicory, and dandelion leaves), whole-grain breads, citrus fruits, and legumes all contain high concentrations of folic acid. Many foods rich in iron and protein also contain folic acid.

Salt and Fats. It used to be that a pregnant woman was put on a low-salt diet, but these days a moderate amount of salt is not only considered safe but encouraged. And while a diet for a woman carrying multiples may appear to be high in fat, fat is important in the absorption of vitamins and minerals. Don't shy away from dairy products because of high fat content—enjoy!

Vitamin Supplements

Taking a prenatal vitamin every day doesn't mean you can skip a meal—it simply offers insurance that every essential vitamin and mineral requirement is covered. Some women carrying twins will be advised by their physicians to take several kinds of supplements (iron, calcium, and so on).

Tips on Gaining Enough Weight

Pregnancy is no time to start a diet, but for some women, consuming more than 3,500 calories each day is the equivalent to standing on one foot while skateboarding—in short, a real challenge. Take mealtime seriously and consider the following tips to help put on the pounds.

- **Make every meal count.** Plan your meals carefully, making sure you eat a wide range of healthy, fresh food with an emphasis on protein. Choose foods that are nutritious, given their calorie and fat content. Sour cream may seem like a delicious way to get a serving of dairy, but check the label—it offers little nutritional value. On the other hand, if you feel your diet is too high in fat, substituting low-fat cottage cheese or 1 percent milk is a better alternative than cutting it out completely.

- **Eat often.** Eating several small meals each day instead of three large ones will keep your energy level high, offer a constant flow of nutrients to growing babies, and eliminate that uncomfortable "stuffed" feeling often associated with eating a large meal. Shoot for seven small meals a day—breakfast, midmorning snack, lunch, midafternoon snack, dinner, bedtime snack, and, finally, a potty-break-in-the-middle-of-the-night snack. (Have a small snack tray of fruit slices, cheese, or peanut butter and crackers by your bed so that when you get up in the middle of the night to use the bathroom, you can grab a quick bite.)

- **Increase dairy foods.** Because they are high in protein, calcium, and calories, dairy foods are a quick answer to fulfilling extra caloric and protein requirements.

- **Drink liquids with calories.** Substitute broths, fresh fruit juices, or milk for your eight glasses of water each day.

- **Bag it.** Whether it's a short trip to the supermarket or an afternoon drive in the country, be sure to keep a supply of nutritious snacks in the car, in your handbag, and in your office drawer. Never be without a secret stash of food!

- **Accessorize your food.** Grated cheese or chopped roasted peanuts sprinkled on a salad add not only flavor but a nice little protein kick.

- **Disguise foods you dislike.** Can't stand eggs or milk? Hide them in delicious dishes like creamed soups, cream sauces, French toast, or even chocolate milk.

Importance of Fluids

Not only is getting enough food important for a woman expecting twins, so is drinking enough fluids. Drinking at least eight glasses of liquid a day eases constipation and reduces the risk of a urinary tract infection. Your body needs the extra fluid to help transport nutrients to your babies, build cells, and remove waste from both your system and the babies'. The added fluid builds additional blood, amniotic fluid, and tissue.

Cut out the Caffeine

Through the years, women have heard conflicting news reports on whether caffeine will increase their chances of miscarriage. During 2008, however, evidence has come to light strongly suggesting that cutting out the stimulant altogether during pregnancy is a good idea. Researchers at Kaiser Permanente Division of Research found that women who consumed about 200 milligrams of caffeine (that's about two cups of coffee) a day doubled their risk of having a miscarriage. Furthermore, even women who consumed less than 200 milligrams a day had a 40 percent chance of miscarriage. Although some say more research needs to be done, err on the side of caution and try a cup of herbal tea. (I drank a cup of hot water in the morning. Not quite the same, but it gave me the illusion of that earthy cup of joe.)

Taboos

The dangers of smoking have been known for years, but the hazards of tobacco are magnified even more during pregnancy. Not only does smoking while pregnant put your life at risk by increasing your chances for heart disease and cancer, but it also has been associated with low birth weight, placenta previa, miscarriages, sudden infant death syndrome (SIDS), and even preterm labor.

Another taboo to avoid during pregnancy is alcohol. Women who drink regularly during pregnancy often have children with fetal alcohol syndrome, a serious condition that includes mental retardation, growth deficiencies, and abnormalities. Various conflicting reports on how much alcohol during pregnancy is safe are inconclusive—so once again, a pregnant mom should err on the side of caution and omit alcohol completely from her lifestyle.

And of course, the use of illegal drugs such as marijuana and cocaine are potential time bombs to a pregnant woman. Avoid them at all costs.

Tips for Increasing Chances of a Healthy Pregnancy

- **Diet.** Follow a healthy diet high in calcium, iron, folic acid, and especially protein. Vary your food consumption to be sure that you're getting a variety of nutrients, and eat plenty of fresh fruits and vegetables. Shoot for a 40 to 45 pound weight gain—gaining the majority of weight by Week 28. And don't forget—protein, protein, protein. The more the better. So think meat, chicken, fish, beans, and dairy.

- **Rest.** Don't wait until your doctor puts you on mandatory bed rest— rest often by either napping frequently or putting your feet up for 30 minutes at least three times a day.

- **Prenatal care.** Never miss a doctor's appointment. Read everything you can on multiple pregnancies. Ask questions and discuss your concerns with your physician.

- **Fluids.** Drink, drink, drink, and then drink more (water, juice, and milk).

- **Precautions.** Don't wait until you're exhausted to rest or starving to eat. Use your common sense when it comes to caring for your body. Avoid alcohol, don't smoke or take any kind of drugs, and always wear your seatbelt while driving. To avoid unnecessary radiation, sit at least 10 feet from the television and stay away from microwave ovens that are in use.

- **Body language.** No one knows the patient better than you. Learn to listen to your body and promptly respond to its needs.

One Final Thought

Being pregnant with twins takes a lot of work and diligence on your part to ensure a healthy outcome, but it's just nature's way of mentally preparing you for what lies ahead. After the birth of your twins, you'll soon realize that pregnancy was the easy part.

•3•

It's All in the Planning

"Why do it today when you can put it off until tomorrow?" While this sentiment is typically the battle cry for busy parents, expectant parents of twins should take the opposite approach—do it now or you may never get it done! Around the seventh month of pregnancy, start thinking about setting up your nursery. Shop early for clothes and furniture just in case your little bundles of joy arrive sooner than expected. If your home needs some alterations to accommodate two extra people (as ours did), don't wait until your babies are tucked snugly in their cribs before you start getting contract bids. Plan ahead and you'll be all the happier for it.

Nursery Essentials

Two of everything? Many parents of twins say, "not necessarily." Before you break the bank with needless infant equipment, it makes better economic sense to buy only one of all the baby extras, like swings and snugly sacks, and then wait and see how your babies respond to each. This way you won't be stuck with more than you need. If, for instance, you find by the second week that you can't survive without two swings, buy another. The exception to this rule, however, is vibrating bouncer seats. This was by far the number one item parents of twins say they couldn't live without, with several parents telling me that they bought four—two for upstairs and a set for downstairs.

CRIB

Probably the most important piece
of equipment, the crib is the
focal point of every
nursery. No need to
buy or borrow two right
away—twins can easily
sleep together for the first
six months (and sometimes
longer). When your babies
begin to roll and move (about
four months of age), however, you
will need to take steps to deter them
from disturbing each other's sleep. A rolled-up blanket or padded bumper (available through catalogs and some baby stores) anchored down the center of the crib keeps everyone on his or her own side. With the recent rise in twinning, some companies are even manufacturing compact double cribs (an Internet search reveals many options).

BOUNCER SEATS

For those moments between feeding, sleeping, and cuddling, bouncer seats are a great place for babies to check out their new world while parents catch their breaths. Some seats have vibrating motors that gently soothe babies to sleep (my kids spent many a night in theirs).

CAR SEATS

By law, each twin needs his or her own car seat while riding in an automobile. Infants weighing up to 20 pounds need a rear-facing seat, while toddlers weighing 20 to 40 pounds require a front-facing car seat. After 40 pounds many states mandate that a child be restrained up to age eight (or 80 pounds) using a booster seat, a change from the old rule of age six (or 60 pounds). Styles and prices range dramatically, but to save money, consider buying a car seat that converts from rear-facing to front-facing. If you purchase this dual model, you'll only need to buy two seats instead of four. There is a drawback, however. If you buy front-facing seats, you'll also need to buy infant carriers to help you transport your babies in and out of the house. (Big and bulky, front-facing seats aren't portable.) Rear-facing car seats are small, easy to remove from the car, and can act as infant carriers, enabling one parent to transport both babies from the house to the car in one trip—an important consideration when the parent is alone and doesn't want to leave a baby unattended. In addition, rear-facing models allow parents to take snoozing infants directly from the car into restaurants and such without removing them from their seats and disturbing their slumber.

STROLLERS

What was the number one item that expectant parents of twins researched to death? The double stroller. And for good reason since they spent a lot of time pushing it, folding and unfolding it, and heaving it in and out of their car trunks. Years ago, parents expecting twins had a difficult time locating a double stroller. These days, however, choices abound. The tandem stroller where one baby sits in front of the other makes maneuvering through doorways easy. But there are a few drawbacks—only the baby in back can fully recline for a nap on the go; the baby in front is left to nap in a semi-upright position. Many parents with twins told me that they quickly gave up the tandem stroller for that very reason. Also, some twins like to kick and bother the passenger in front.

Side-by-side strollers, on the other hand, are lighter and more compact than the tandem style, but many don't offer enough back support for tiny infants. In addition, tight store aisles as well as doorways sometimes pose a maneuverability problem. In recent years, jogging strollers have grown very popular. Babies sit side by side and with bigger wheels, the jogger handles all types of terrain—rocky soil, snow, and ice. These strollers maneuver great, and now many manufacturers are making them narrow enough to fit through standard doorways. Drawbacks? They're a bit bulky, heavy, and very expensive (although one mom told me she resold hers after her twins outgrew it and easily got half of what she paid for it).

The parents that I interviewed all had unique ways of conducting their own marketing research when it came to deciding on a stroller. One mom took her four-year-old son to the store and had him sit in a variety of different models and then tell her which ones were most comfortable; another mom stopped other parents wheeling twins around the shopping mall to ask them what they thought of the model they had. (For a list of their favorite picks, check out the sidebar, Top Five Twin Gadgets, later in this chapter.)

Before you pay the big bucks for a stroller, decide how you'll use it. Will you be a mom on the go, power walking around the neighborhood? Then maybe a jogger is for you. Or will you be lugging it in and out of the car every day as you run errands around town? Then perhaps a lightweight tandem is the better fit. Test-drive a few models in the store to see how they handle cornering. But most important—is it easy to fold and unfold, is it light enough to lift by yourself, and will it fit into the trunk of your car?

SWING

A lifesaver for many parents, a swing gently calms even the fussiest baby. But should you purchase two? Considering the expense (swings run anywhere from $60 to $200) and space, many parents say no. Instead, buy one now and take a wait-and-see approach. (Some parents, like myself, never purchased a swing with no ill effects.)

CLOTHING

Although most friends and family will give you clothes in duplicate, your twins' wardrobe need not be twice that of a single baby. Each needs a personal jacket, shoes, and hat, but they can share play clothes and pajamas. One mom who received an enormous amount of clothing from baby showers, told me, "Don't take the tags off! They won't wear half of it." Instead, snip as you go and in a few months if you find their closet filled with unworn clothing that they've now outgrown, sell it all on EBay. For moms trolling the Internet for deals, "new with tags" (NWT) sell big on the auction website.

BLANKETS

Infants require plenty of blankets—light cotton for swaddling (three to four each), wool afghan for strolling (two each), soft flannel to place on the floor for playtime (one each), and colorful receiving blankets (one each). While 14–16 blankets may seem too many, it will save you from having to do laundry every day.

TOYS

For the first six months, most babies don't have much interest in toys, but around four months of age they will enjoy batting at a play gym. You'll need only one—babies are small enough to be placed side by side underneath.

Top Five Wardrobe Essentials
and Expendables

Once the baby shower is over, take inventory of your twins' wardrobe and fill in those gaping fashion holes before your babies arrive. But shop carefully—baby clothes are expensive.

1. **Essential: one-piece stretch suits.** During the first few weeks, make life easy on yourself and dress babies in comfortable cotton stretch suits. They'll keep your little ones warm, they launder great, they have no clumsy buttons or zippers, plus they're inexpensive.

2. **Expendable: matching outfits.** Okay, maybe just one set for that special first photograph, but for everyday wear, matching outfits are a waste of money.

3. **Essential: cotton onesies.** Perfect if you live in a warm climate or your babies are born in the summer, these one-piece T-shirts are cool, crisp, and comfortable.

4. **Expendable: booties and mittens.** "Newborn shoes were a waste of money," one mom said. "They just kick them off. And I stayed at home so much in the beginning that I had no use for them." If you take your twins out in cool weather, just dress them in one-piece stretch suits and then wrap them snugly in wool blankets.

5. **Essential: hats.** Protect delicate bald heads and necks from the sun with brimmed hats.

Diapers

Count on using about 150 diapers a week for the first few months. But should you use cloth or disposable diapers? Each has its benefits and pitfalls.

Advantages of Cloth Diapers

- Environmentally, cloth is the winner. Before they are toilet trained, your twins will use 17,000 to 25,000 diapers. That's a lot of trash!

- Most services deliver fresh cloth diapers every week directly to your door so you'll never run out.

- Cloth diapers breathe, preventing diaper rash.

- Babies who wear cloth diapers toilet train sooner.

Disadvantages of Cloth Diapers

- You must purchase plastic covers at a cost of $5 each (you'll need at least five for each baby). And as your babies grow, you'll need to purchase larger sizes.

- They are not as absorbent as disposables and often shift inside their covers, leading to messy leaks and countless daily cleanups.

Advantages of Disposables

- They are easy to use—no diaper folding or Velcro covers involved.

- They're more absorbent, which is especially helpful at night or when traveling.

Disadvantages of Disposables

- Disposables create an excessive amount of garbage both in your home and in our nation's burgeoning landfills.

- The plastic outer lining doesn't breathe. Couple that with excess moisture buildup due to their absorbability and the result for most babies is a nasty diaper rash.

Most parents say the cost comparison balances out. While the unit cost per cloth diaper is cheaper than disposables, cloth requires more frequent changing. In addition, parents with twins need to buy at least 10 covers ($50) every few months as their babies grow. (Although to combat the landfill crisis, some city municipalities are offering cloth diaper coupons and discounts to their customers!) Looking for a compromise? Use cloth during the day while at home and then switch to disposables for outings and nighttime.

Baby Monitor

Not just for nighttime, baby monitors permit mobility—a must for housebound parents. While the twins nap, take the monitor outside and do a little gardening or relax in the sunshine. It'll feel like a mini-vacation.

Snugly Sack

Single or double, a snugly sack is worn across your chest, keeping baby close and happy and your hands free. It's a must for anyone with a fussy baby yet who needs to get the chores done.

Playpen/Port-a-Crib/Pack-n-Play

A pack-n-play (also known as a port-a-crib) is a safe haven to place a calm baby while you soothe a not-so-calm twin. Or use it as a play area while doing another load of laundry. Don't expect to use it as a playpen past the first year, though. Once they become mobile, most babies protest when placed inside. But it's still a useful investment if you're a family on the go. A playpen is lightweight and compact, and therefore useful as a crib for overnight traveling. Many families use the pack-n-play for a secondary spot for their twins to nap, and they are so convenient that some parents even invest in two and use the second one in another part of the house.

Don't Waste Your Money

It may have sounded like a good idea at the time but once they bought a product, it just sat in the corner not being used. Here are some things that parents with newborn twins thought were a waste of money. The Diaper Genie ("Doesn't fit many diapers; too costly to keep buying refill bags.") topped many lists, followed by bottle warmers ("By the time it took to heat the bottles up in the middle of the night, my boys were hysterical. Canned formula or a pitcher of room temperature water to mix with the powdered formula worked best."), and finally, the plastic bathtub. ("It was easier to fill the hospital basin up and sponge bathe them when they were newborn, and when they could sit, I bathed them in the kitchen sink. It was the right height, and all you have to do is pull a drain when you are done.")

FUTURE NURSERY ITEMS

No need to buy everything before the babies arrive. Many nursery items aren't necessary until twins reach six months or older.

High Chairs or Hook-on Chairs

Once the twins start on solid foods at six months, it's time to think about high chairs. Some parents opt for one and feed their babies in shifts. Instead, we chose to buy two hook-on chairs (small, folding chairs that clamp directly onto a table, sometimes called "tot-locks"). They're less expensive (around $35 for a hook-on chair versus $100 for a high chair), they save space (a big consideration for my cramped residence), and they're portable. Since we took these chairs everywhere, we never had to worry about finding two high chairs when we went to a restaurant or visit family.

Umbrella Strollers/Travel Strollers

When twins begin to walk, many rebel against sitting in their double stroller—it's too confining. Two single umbrella or travel strollers offer a solution by allowing babies to sit upright in full view of everything. Umbrella strollers are also more compact than double strollers, making them perfect for traveling. Some parents find that buying two single strollers allows for various combinations: one parent, one twin; two parents, two twins; one parent, two twins (one in stroller, one in backpack; or clamp them together with stroller clips or stroller connectors—available online—to make a double stroller).

Two for the Price of One? Money Matters

For families who are suddenly surprised to find that two babies are on the way instead of just one, saving money becomes a major priority. And while it will ultimately cost more to raise twins (start those 529 college savings accounts now!), the good news is that there are ways for parents of multiples to make their pennies go further.

When we first learned that we were having twins, my pragmatic husband quipped, "Will we get a deal on our hospital bill?" Actually,

TOP FIVE TWIN GADGETS

Just like professional chefs, families with twins know that the secret to success is in the tools they use. Here's a nursery list of five favorites to help life run more smoothly.

1. **Double stroller.** These three top most everyone's list—Mountain Buggy Urban Double Jogging Stroller, the tandem Graco Duo-Glide, and the side-by-side Combi double stroller.

2. **Boppy pillow.** This horseshoe-shaped pillow holds babies upright—perfect for bottle feeding or when babies just want to hang out and watch their surroundings. ("I couldn't have lived without our Boppy. I would prop the girls up in them and feed both at the same time on the couch.")

3. **Baby sling or carrier.** Whether a single carrier like the Baby-Björn Baby Carrier or the Sleepy Wrap Baby Carrier that can even hold twins up to Month 3, or double carriers like the Weego Twin Baby Carrier or the MaxiMom Twin Carrier, moms agree—they love having babies close but also having moms' hands free.

4. **Nursing pillow.** If you plan on breastfeeding, you definitely need a nursing pillow so you can tandem nurse. The Viva Nursing Pillow offers plenty of room for two plus back support for mom.

5. **Miracle Blanket.** Moms swear by the Miracle Blanket's calming effect even on the fussiest baby. ("Babies love to be swaddled, and this blanket swaddles them about as tight as you can get and doesn't come loose. And they fit in it until they were about four months old!")

the answer is yes and no. Physicians do charge more for a twin delivery than a singleton delivery, but the cost for prenatal visits and delivery is not double the price. The amount of your hospital room will remain the same as that for a singleton delivery, but your nursery bill and pediatrician visits will cost double.

When looking into day-care centers, mommy-and-me classes, and even preschool, it's a nice surprise to learn that many offer a discount (between 10 and 20 percent) when enrolling a second child at the same time. So you see, it does pay to have twins!

Reevaluate Your Budget

Before you completely give up your weekly night out with your spouse in an effort to save some cash, consider reevaluating some fixed expenses in your family budget. First, think about refinancing your mortgage. Even if you can shave off only 1 percent, it could be worth hundreds of dollars annually if you're planning on staying in your present home for more than a few years. And did you know that nearly one-third of American homes are assessed higher than their worth, resulting in a needlessly higher tax bill? If you feel that your house is overvalued, call your county tax assessor for a reassessment. You may also save 10 to 20 percent a year on homeowners and auto insurance by simply raising your deductible to $500 or $1,000.

Even small cuts in the budget add up to big savings over time. Instead of giving up cable altogether, cut out the premium channels and get a basic package instead. Do you only use your cell phone for quick calls or just emergencies? Then drop your month-to-month plan and sign up for a pay-as-you-go plan. This type of plan works like a debit card—you refill your account with minutes every 90 days and just pay for the minutes you use. Another idea is to buy inexpensive phone cards at warehouse stores where you'll pay about three cents a minute (taxes included) for long distance calls you make from home.

DOUBLE-DUTY ITEMS

With a little imagination, you'd be surprised at what you can use in multiple ways. Forget about a portable plastic tub or tub ring—try bathing babies in the kitchen sink. When they outgrow the sink, place small, square laundry baskets in the bathtub and put babies inside. The water flows freely through the baskets while keeping babies in an upright position. When the twins are old enough to sit in the tub on their own, use the baskets for toy chests or what they were created for—laundry.

Thinking of buying a changing table? How about spreading a large towel on the floor or on top of a bed instead? We saved money by buying a thick changing pad and placing it on top of our dresser. If you need to furnish your home, think about buying baby furniture with a future. What will you do with the $200 changing table in two years? Probably store it in the attic for the next 20. An antique dry sink (look in the newspaper or scour flea markets or secondhand furniture stores) padded with colorful baby bumpers works just as well, and in a few years you'll have a lovely piece of furniture to use in another part of your home. Instead of a brightly painted nursery rocker, we bought a more mainstream mission-style rocking chair that now sits proudly in our living room.

BREASTFEEDING

Not only is breastfeeding better for your babies, it also saves lots of money. The average newborn drinks $80 to $100 worth of formula each month depending on brand. Multiply that by two and you have enough for a car payment (and a new, bigger car might come in handy now).

DO IT YOURSELF

Good with a needle and thread? Why not sew your own baby bumpers and crib blankets? When it's time to introduce solid foods to your twins, make your own baby food. While it's much easier just to open a jar (and on many a tired evening I did), you'll save plenty by making your own. Check out your local bookstore or library for parenting books that contain simple recipes.

Save more money by making your own baby wipes. Start with a roll of top-quality paper towels, baby oil, water, and a round plastic container with a lid. With a sharp knife, slice the towel roll into two equal halves. Place one-half in the plastic container and store the second half for future use. Slowly drizzle ⅓ cup baby oil evenly on top of the towels and then add 2 cups water. Seal the container for approximately one hour to aid in the absorption. If the towels are too dry, add a few tablespoons of water; if too moist, simply leave the lid off for an hour or two.

After dropping more than $50 to get my young twins' hair cut, I learned to do it myself (and I'm pretty good at it, too). The instructional video that came with the electric buzzer that I bought showed me the basics.

Freebies, Coupons, and Discounts

Many corporations, like Gerber, Beechnut, and Kimberly Clark, offer coupons and free samples of baby food, diapers, and formula to families with multiples (for a complete list, see the Appendix). Many national chains, such as Babies R Us, OshKosh, and Stride Rite shoes, also offer discounts to families of multiples. One mom urged, "No matter where you go, ask if they offer a discount for twins!" Many stores offer discounts but don't advertise the fact. Another mom swears by shopping websites such as thegrocerygame.com and coupons.com while many families stock up on staples such as diapers and jarred baby food at discount warehouse stores, including Costco, BJs, or Sam's Club. But it's always best to comparison shop first before you pay big bucks for a case of diapers.

Want to get out of the house with your spouse but concerned about spending money? Many organizations (including Mothers of Twins Clubs) raise money by selling coupon books chock-full of discounts on movie tickets and two-for-one deals at local eateries.

Secondhand Rose

When it was time to get a second crib (our boys shared one crib for the first six months), we hit the used furniture stores. We saved more than 50 percent on a previously owned crib. With a little cleaning, our used crib looked as good as new.

One mom told me she relies on consignment stores for great deals on baby equipment as well as clothes. "I also take our gently used clothing my children have outgrown to a local secondhand store. They give me cash on the spot for all the items I bring in," she said. "I also learned to very graciously accept hand-me-down toys and clothes. In the beginning I wanted everything to be new, but I quickly realized that that was impractical. Now hand-me-downs are treated like gold around here."

Join your local Mothers of Twins Club (log on to nomotc.org for a list of such clubs in the United States; amba.org.au in Australia; tamba. org.uk in Great Britain, or multiplebirthscanada.org in Canada) and reap the benefits of their semiannual twin clothing sales. Some sales are so big and popular, the clubs rent out local auditoriums. One mom told me she not only bought clothing and equipment through her local twins' club sale but sold the items that her twins ultimately outgrew. "They use everything so quickly that it becomes a waste of space after six months. My club's sale was like a big rental service to me," she explained. "I'd buy something, clean it, and then use it for six months. Then I'd sell it at the next sale usually for the same amount or a little less. So my boys had new toys all the time."

One More Thing . . .

Don't get stuck on name brands, which are often expensive, when store brands will do the same trick. Shop for off-season home furnishings and clothing—think outdoor furniture in September and winter coats in March (just be sure to buy a size up). Know how much things cost, and remember that a sale isn't always a bargain. And finally, one mom told me that she gives very specific details to family members when they ask what to get her babies. ("They need four pairs of size 18-month pajamas, short sleeve.") In the end, with a little common sense and some careful planning, having twins doesn't have to send you to the poorhouse.

Getting the Family Ready for Twins

The crib is in place, the curtains are hung—now what? Start by making a list of what you'd like to have done before the babies' arrival. Everyone's priorities are different, but here are a few ideas to get you started.

The Birth Experience

Things begin to heat up in your second trimester. Not only will you begin to see your doctor more often, but now you'll really start to slow down due to your increasing size. It's really going to happen—you're going to give birth to two! To that end, you'll need to prepare for their birth.

Enroll in Childbirth Classes

Whether you choose Lamaze, Bradley, or Grantly Dick-Read, childbirth classes help expectant moms (and dads) ease the fear and pain of childbirth through knowledge and relaxation techniques. Instructors also speak on prenatal education, and participants are encouraged to voice concerns and ask questions. While most parents expecting a singleton take the class during the eighth month of pregnancy, book yours earlier just in case the kids make an unscheduled arrival. With the influx of twin births, many hospitals are offering childbirth classes specifically for parents expecting multiples. Several moms told me that they attended such a class but felt that the twin-specific information offered wasn't worth the trouble—a good book like the one in your hands worked just as well.

Take CPR

Taking an infant cardiopulmonary resuscitation (CPR) class not only prepares you for an emergency, but gives you the confidence you'll need if your babies are born prematurely and suffer from apnea. Contact your local hospital or Red Cross for a list of class locations.

Tour the Hospital

Call the hospital where you'll be giving birth to set up a tour. Usually offered in the evenings, the tour will give you a sense of familiarity and help to ease your anxieties when the big day arrives. You'll have plenty of opportunity to ask questions. And remember to ask to see the NICU.

Make a Birth Plan

Although your birth plan will probably change many times during the course of labor (pain has a way of transforming even the meekest woman into a bossy tyrant), it's important to have a vision of how you want your labor and subsequent delivery to go. That's where a birth plan comes in. It's a written statement expressing your wishes and includes everything from lighting (soft and subtle or bright and energizing) to the amount of people present at the birth (just your hubby or a doula and other family members). Birth plans are important since there are so many details to the birth experience, and the last thing a woman in labor wants to do is change her focus and make dozens of decisions. For instance, you should decide beforehand if you'd like pain medication. Your birth plan should also include the labor positions you'd like to try (do you want to walk or lie on your side, for instance), and even if you'd like to avoid episiotomy.

If you don't know how to express your wishes as eloquently as you'd like, do a Google search of "birth plans" and you'll find simple online forms. It's a good idea to make three separate plans: one for a vaginal delivery, one for a cesarean delivery, and one for a premature delivery, since all three are possible.

Select a Pediatrician

The relationship between you and your pediatrician is an important one. Your twins will visit him or her at least six to eight times during the first year of life (more if they get sick). To find a reliable candidate, begin the process in your seventh month and ask friends with kids or contact your local Mothers of Twins Club for recommendations. Many local hospitals offer a doctor referral line, and the American Academy of Pediatrics (aap.org) has a database of local doctors as well. Since twins have a higher chance of visiting the doctor more often than singletons simply because there are two of them, be sure to choose a pediatrician close to home. After you've selected two or three prospects, make sure your candidates are covered by your insurance policy and then set up a get-acquainted appointment where you can meet the doctor and ask questions. Don't overlook this simple step as it's important to feel comfortable with your children's doctor. You'll be asking many questions on a host of subjects from eating and sleeping issues to vaccinations and blood tests schedules. Some physicians charge for this get-acquainted appointment, but many insurance companies will pick up the tab.

Cook Ahead

During those first chaotic weeks after the babies are born, cooking will be the last thing on your mind. (Okay, making love will be the last thing on your mind, but cooking runs a close second-to-last.) But you

Top Five Essential Items to Take to the Hospital

Your favorite nightgown, your Frank Sinatra CD, and baby clothes. What else do you need? Plenty. Be prepared with this list of must-have gear.

1. **Food for Dad.** Don't overlook the coach. Since hospital cafeterias close early and labor could happen at 2 A.M., pack a small cooler with sandwiches, fruit, and beverages. (Just try not to get too mad when he's chowing down while you're panting between contractions.)

2. **Insurance cards, checkbook, and emergency cash.** You might be concentrating on the birth, but some hospital administrators are concerned with paperwork. Don't be caught off-guard.

3. **The good news list.** After the excitement and exhaustion of giving birth, you won't remember the people you have to call. Make a list of names and phone numbers in descending order from most important—Grandma and Grandpa—to the "maybe laters," like Great-Aunt Lucy in Topeka.

4. **Extra batteries.** Whether it's for a flash camera or a portable tape player, have plenty of batteries packed (hospitals don't allow you to plug any electronic equipment into their outlets).

5. **Play things.** Believe it or not, sometimes there's a little downtime during labor. It's best to keep yourself (and your partner) occupied by playing cards, reading a book, or playing a game.

still have to eat, right? Having dinner in the freezer all ready to go will be the best gift you can give yourself. Take a few weekends before the birth of the babies and cook a variety of meals that you can dole out in family-size portions and freeze. Have a friend or family member come on over to give you a hand. (It's hard to move around a kitchen with a big belly.) Several moms told me how grateful they were to their own mothers, fathers, and in-laws who came over a few weeks before the birth to cook and freeze meals. "My mother-in-law visited the week before the babies came and froze a bunch of meals for us," said one mom. "That really helped out, and what a treat!" In another family, the husband's colleagues graciously organized a meal rotation during the first month.

If you're up to cooking and freezing, stick to easy, one-pot dinners such as beef stew, lasagna, and chicken potpie. And while you're at it, stock the pantry too, with staples like pasta, rice, beans, jarred sauces, and condiments.

S.O.S.—Getting Help

Take people up on their offer to help. Find out ahead of time which people are baby people and which people just want to do laundry or cook. If they really want to help in some way, they'll appreciate being asked. Don't underestimate the help of young neighborhood kids who love to feed and hold babies. They're great stroller pushers, too!

Toward the end of my pregnancy, the size of my belly drew a lot of attention and many unwanted comments. The most common, "Will you have help?" always puzzled me. *Why does everyone think I'll need help? I can handle two babies easily,* I thought. I imagined two docile infants either sleeping or cooing happily. Endless diaper changes, fussing, and colic never entered my mind. Looking back, I realize that I was lost in a prenatal fantasy. Fortunately, I woke up just in time to recruit a close network of family and friends before the birth, and I strongly advise you to do the same.

Nearly all the families interviewed for this book had some form of assistance during the first two months. Some hired night nurses or postpartum doulas who came to the house a few hours a week. One family even researched and hired an *au pair* from Poland. Overwhelmingly, though, most families relied on their own parents for help. A few had parents and in-laws literally move in for the first few months! But most simply had an entourage of family members just a phone call away. "We had my mother and sisters, his mother and sister," explained one mom. "To this day the boys' grandmothers still watch them on a weekly basis. It's been a godsend to have these two wonderful women to help us with child care."

Yet for some parents whose families live too far away to pitch in daily or who simply can't afford to hire help, what options do they have? Some moms chose to hire a less expensive "mother's helper," a neighborhood teen in need of a small job after school. While the moms weren't confident in leaving their helpers alone in the house with their new babies, the sitters were able to entertain the twins for a few hours, giving moms some time off in another room.

"I had a neighbor's 10-year-old come over and help with dinnertime," one mom said. "She would feed the boys in the high chairs while I got the other kids sorted. Then she'd help out with the baths, which was great. She loved helping."

Another alternative is to enlist the help of friends. I was blessed with three terrific friends who used vacation or sick days at work and came over twice a week for the first two months. They did my laundry, washed dishes, cooked dinner, cuddled my kids, and offered plenty of loving support. At first I felt guilty, but I gave in to their pampering and enjoyed the indulgence. Once I got my new life under control, I pampered them a little by treating them to a special lunch at a favorite restaurant.

PREPARING OLDER CHILDREN

Elizabeth knew it in her head but like us was not prepared emotionally for the reality of not having Mommy to herself anymore or for the general increase in noise that two younger siblings bring. It really hit home when she was in kindergarten and had to make a magic wand for a school project. She could have written any wish on the wand. While her classmates wished for ponies or trips to Disneyland, Elizabeth wished for "pease and qwiet."

With all the prenatal arrangements and ensuing excitement, older children often get lost in the shuffle. Seventeen families interviewed for this book faced the sometimes difficult challenge of trying to prepare older children for the arrival of not one but two younger siblings.

Parents with older children agree that talking on a daily basis about the arrival of the twins and what that would mean to all their lives helped but most admitted that the concept was hard for a young child to grasp. "One can only explain so much to a three-year-old," a mom explained. If you know of another family with twins (and these days, who doesn't?) try to arrange a play date so that your child can see and understand what a twin actually is. Some parents bought their older children twin dolls; others read children's books centering on the arrival of twins.

Many parents got their older children involved. Some took them to their prenatal visits where they were able to hear the fetal heartbeats. Whether you're cooking meals to freeze or deciding on nursery wallpaper, children love to help. Let them have some say in the decision-making process. All this hands-on assistance helps children feel invested in the arrival of their new siblings. "I had my boys be responsible for very simple things so they felt part of the arrival of twins," one mom said. "For example, when I gave the twins a bath, I had them be responsible for bringing me a towel. My oldest loved turning on the baby monitor for me. I explained to him that this was an important job since I needed to be able to hear the twins when they cried."

Before the babies arrive, curl up on the couch, open up your children's baby books, and reminisce with them about the day they were born. Look at their baby pictures, their first tooth, their hospital bracelet, and so on, and reassure them that you will still love and care for them after the arrival of their new siblings. Although what you do and say before the arrival of twins is important, your behavior and attitude toward your singleton is even more important after the birth of multiples. Try to find a way to spend one-on-one time alone each day with your older children doing something that they choose, whether reading a story or playing a game.

If you're going to have a family friend take care of your children while you're away at the hospital, introduce the new sitter to your children now. Let them get acquainted and feel comfortable with each other weeks before the birth. If you're going to move bedrooms around to make room for the babies, make sure to do it very early in the pregnancy so your children don't feel as though they were put out of their own room.

And, finally, don't forget about preparing the family pet. One mom took the advice of her veterinarian and primed her puppy by periodically tugging gently on his tail and ears to simulate the pulls of a toddler. "Once the girls were born but still in the hospital, we'd bring home items that they'd worn and let him smell them," she explained. "And it worked. My dog is perfect with my girls."

TOP FIVE WAYS TO DEVELOP SIBLING BONDS

Helping kids make the transition from only child to older sister or brother doesn't end when the twins are born. Parents should encourage a healthy bond daily to avoid resentment among all.

1. **Stress ownership.** Explain to your kids that they're getting a set of new sisters or brothers rather than saying that Mommy and Daddy are having babies. By stressing ownership, older children will feel like their new siblings are a gift rather than a burden.

2. **Encourage activities together.** While you shouldn't force your child to play with his or her new siblings, think of activities that they can all do together like reading, singing, watching a movie, or building with blocks.

3. **Intervene in public.** Be prepared for lots of "oohs" and "ahs" from strangers directed at your twins. Don't let your older child feel left out. If a stranger remarks on your twins' beautiful hair, chime in with: "Yes, they get it from their older sister, Nancy."

4. **Respect privacy.** Older children often resent their younger twin siblings for invading their space. Set firm ground rules with your twins about what toys are off-limits or when their older sibling can't be bothered.

5. **Avoid the nanny role.** While it's tempting to use your older children as built-in babysitters or mother's helpers, keep this role to a minimum—otherwise they may resent, rather than cherish, their new roles as older siblings.

Taking Care of Business

During the first few months after the twins arrive, there isn't much time to take a shower let alone handle all the household paperwork. Take care of business now while you still can.

Enroll in Online Bill Pay

If you don't have your paychecks direct-deposited or you haven't registered to pay your bills online, sign up now. It saves an enormous amount of time—no standing in line at the bank, no checks to fill out, and no frantically looking for postage. You can even automate your monthly bills. Just pick a day of the month to pay, say, your mortgage, and the bank will automatically withdraw the money from your savings or checking account and send the payment to your mortgage company.

Contact La Leche and Twins Clubs

Make contacts at La Leche (llli.org), and drop in at a local Mothers of Twins Club meeting before the birth of your babies. La Leche offers tips on breastfeeding as well as online forums. Twins clubs, on the other hand, can offer great support for parents of multiples since every one of their parents has been in your shoes! Nearly every mom that I interviewed was grateful for joining their local club whether it was for twin-specific tips, the twice-yearly clothing and equipment sales, or just meeting other moms who "get it."

Set up Diaper Service

If cloth diapers are for you, call and set up an account with your local diaper service.

Get Ready for Thank You, Thank You, Thank You

Before the flood of baby gifts arrive, purchase thank-you notes, select birth announcements, and address the envelopes. And don't forget to have enough postage on hand.

Prepare for Christmas in July

Don't let your older child's birthday get lost in the newborn shuffle. Look ahead four to six months to upcoming holidays and events. If necessary, go Christmas or back-to-school shopping now. And while you're at it, stockpile a supply of emergency birthday party gifts or greet-ing cards on hand, too, so you're never caught empty-handed.

HOW ARE YOU FEELING, HONEY?

Every Friday evening right after work and with cocktails in hand, my husband and I sit on the couch for our weekly "How's it goin'?" session. Whether we talk about our fears, our future goals, or simply how our days went, these discussions have kept us in tune with each other through the years. During my pregnancy, for instance, I learned about my husband's anxiety concerning supporting his growing family (not uncommon for dads-to-be) and his apprehension about becoming a first-time father. Keeping the lines of communication open during pregnancy helps to ease the stress after the babies arrive.

CHOOSING NAMES

My husband and I had a hard enough time deciding on just one name, let alone two. But one thing we did both agree on—we didn't want our sons' names to be similar in any way.

Importance of Names

> We didn't want their names to start with the same letter to avoid insurance confusion. We just wanted two, somewhat traditional names that could be shortened and sounded good together. My husband decided early on that whoever was born first would have the name that came second alphabetically. His reasoning? Zack can always say he is older, but Nick will graduate first!

My fraternal boys look nothing alike, yet family members and friends who didn't see them frequently during the first year often mixed them up. It's easier for people to group twins together and see them as a unit rather than as individuals. Giving each twin a distinct name, therefore, separates them from each other and identifies them as individual peo-ple. Dissimilar names shout out to the world, "I may be a twin, but I am unique."

Problems with Similar-Sounding Names

Choosing names like Tom and Tim or Amanda and Amy presents prob-lems for family and friends trying to distinguish between the children.

(One mom wisely pointed out that alliterating names limited her choices.) In addition, names with the same first initial will undoubtedly create problems down the road concerning recordkeeping as well as mail. Stay away from "couple" names like Bonnie and Clyde, Anthony and Cleopatra, and the like, which may seem cute at birth but will surely be resented by your children as they enter school. "Theme" names like Daisy and Iris or Hope and Charity reinforce unit thinking as well and should be avoided. Remember, your kids must live with the names that you have chosen for them, so select them wisely.

But from a purely practical perspective, one mom put it this way: "It's been very useful to have names that start with different letters because you wind up labeling everything—bottles, pacifiers, extra clothing for day care, and so on. It's nice to be able to use an initial rather than having to write the whole name."

Amen!

It's Almost Time

Now that your maternity to-do list is quickly dwindling and D-day (delivery day) is rapidly approaching, make an effort to share some special time with your spouse. Do something memorable and out of the ordinary, like going to the opera or dining at a very romantic restaurant. Do it now—you may not get the chance again for a long time.

₀4₀

The First Month: Dirty Little Secrets Parents Won't Tell You

I sometimes didn't even know I was up until I was getting back into bed. It was hard and tiring. My twins didn't look alike to me but at 3 A.M. they started to!

What are the first few months like with newborn twins? To many parents, it remains a mystery. (Sleep deprivation numbs the brain.) While that may be unsettling to expectant parents, the good news is that we all lived through it. Although the first four weeks will seem endless, try to relax and enjoy the crazy ride. Before you know it, they'll be off to college.

Developmental Milestones

What's going on inside a newborn's head? It may not seem like much as your twins peacefully lie in your arms, but during the first month of life your babies will change in many ways. Most babies' reflexes at this early stage are instinctual, like the rooting reflex (where baby turns his or her head toward a specific stimulus). You'll notice the rooting reflex when babies are hungry and they frantically search for your breast. The ability to suck is also instinctual, but babies will, however, stop sucking if they hear something or if an object catches their interest. Another fascinating instinctual movement to watch for is the Moro reflex, where babies fling their arms out and then quickly retract them tightly across their chests. And those peculiar, jerking body movements are also normal and will disappear within a few months.

During the first month, babies will cry often—it's in their job descriptions. Blame it on an immature nervous system, but don't ignore their crying, as they may be hungry or uncomfortable. Sometimes one baby's crying will set off a co-twin, except at night. Strangely, if one twin cries at night, it's rare that the other twin will wake. No need to walk around the house on tiptoes during naptime, either. Newborns block out excessive stimuli by simply falling asleep. (Take advantage of it now and slip out to a restaurant with the twins.) For the next few months they'll continue to sleep in the fetal position—arms and legs tucked close to their bodies. And while it may seem logical to put each baby in his or her own crib, twins often (but not always) quiet down sooner and sleep better when placed together in the same crib. When babies are alert—1 hour for every 10—help jump-start their cognitive development by singing to them, touching them, and offering some large toys to focus on. Although babies can only focus on objects less than 12 inches away, they enjoy studying faces and can even make eye contact.

You'll be amazed at how quickly you'll notice personality differences between your babies (even with identical twins). One will be needier than the other. One might be an excellent nurser while the other may show some reluctance. But don't start labeling their behaviors now. They'll change and flip-flop with each other hundreds of times before their true personalities are set.

Remember that these are just guidelines—some babies will reach these milestones sooner, some later. If your babies were born prematurely, calculate milestones from the due date, not birth date. This is referred to as a twin's "adjusted age."

Keeping Your Head Above Water—First Month Survival Tips

Just as most parents interviewed for this book, I remember little of the first month, and the things that I do recall are not pretty. The night I started lactating, my husband, Kevin, and I stumbled our way to the nursery at 2 A.M. so I could nurse our sons. Back then, Joseph had a difficult time latching on my breast and wailed in frustration every time I tried to nurse him. That night, Kevin looked on helplessly as I sobbed, "He won't eat. I'm starving him!" We felt so desperate that we even tried to feed him using an eyedropper filled with my expressed milk. Joseph was none too pleased with that arrangement either and screamed even louder. Needless to say, it was a very long night.

While you're sure to have plenty of long nights of your own to tell the grandkids about, you can make your life a little easier by following these important tips.

KEEP NOTES

Newborns eat, poop, and pee constantly. And with twins, it's often difficult to remember who did what and when. During the first few days after you bring your babies home, it's important to keep tabs on each baby's nursing/bottle feeding and bowel habits to ensure each is getting enough milk and avoiding dehydration. Keep a notebook in the nursery and chart your twins' habits—who took a bath that day and so on. Keeping notes also eliminates the need to remember the answers to questions the pediatrician is sure to ask, such as "How much are the babies eating?" (You can download a Daily Feeding and Diapering Chart at talk-about-twins.com. It's a helpful tool to keep track of your twins' schedules!)

There are also other ways of keeping a log. Several ingenious parents created spreadsheets on their computers and printed out daily schedules. "It was also very helpful when we had friends and family helping us out for the day. They wrote down what the twins did and there was no confusion later," one mom added.

Joseph

Time	Minutes Nursed or CC Formula	Side	BM	Void	Med/Other
6am	12 min	L	✓	✓	
9:30	20 min	R		✓	
noon	10 min	L		✓	
3pm	20 min	L			
5pm	10 min	R	✓	✓	
7:30p	40 min	L		✓	bath
11pm	25 min	R		✓	
3am	15 min	R		✓	

Michael

Time	Minutes Nursed or CC Formula	Side	BM	Void	Med/Other
6:15a	15 min	R		✓	
9:30	20 min	L		✓	
noon	18 min	R	✓	✓	
3:20p	22 min	R		✓	
5pm	10 min	L		✓	
7:30p	40 min	R	✓		bath
11pm	25 min	L		✓	
3:15a	20 min	L	✓	✓	

TAKE CARE OF YOURSELF

You won't be able to take care of the babies properly unless you take care of yourself. Unfortunately, that sounds so much easier than it is. Eat wholesome, nourishing food, especially if you're nursing. (Now's the time to dip into the freezer for all those great meals you prepared weeks ago.) Remember, what you eat, your babies eat, too. Drink at least eight glasses of liquid each day to keep up your milk supply, and don't forget to continue taking your prenatal vitamins.

SLEEP WHEN YOU CAN

New babies keep odd hours and for the first few weeks, so will you. You'll be up several times a night attending to their demands, so you'll need to catch up on your sleep during the day. Nap when the babies nap, and go to bed when they do.

DON'T ANSWER THE PHONE

Right after our babies were born, we called family and friends telling them the great news, and then we asked them not to call us for a while. During the first month, phone calls were the number one annoyance. Well-meaning folks seem to have a knack for calling right when you've finally gotten the kids (and yourself) down for a nap. Until you're fully rested, don't answer the phone; let the machine get it. If you feel guilty about isolating yourself from your family, send out a short mass e-mail or leave daily messages on your machine updating callers on the progress of your twins.

PRIORITIZE CHORES

If you're one of those people who need to have the bed made every day or the bathroom sparkle, forget it. Let the housework go for a few weeks. Dust bunnies never sent anyone to the hospital. Instead, spend the time catching up on sleep and getting to know your babies. Pick and choose the chores that absolutely need to get done, and leave the rest for another time—like in two years.

LEARN TO TELL YOUR TWINS APART

A dark nursery. Two little bald heads. Who's who? Even parents of fraternal twins have a difficult time telling their infants apart. Try the following tips:

- Keep the hospital ankle tags on for the first few weeks until you can distinguish Baby A from Baby B.

- Color-code their clothing—Baby A wears only blue; Baby B, only yellow. Color-code their car seats, bouncy seats, and even their cribs. Just remember to place the corresponding baby with his or her designated-colored item!

- Apply a touch of nail polish to Baby A's toe.

- Look for a distinguishing feature such as a birthmark. (During the first month, my husband used the shape of our sons' heads to help him tell them apart.)

CREATE BABY STATIONS

Leave plenty of diapers, wipes, and pacifiers at designated points around the house—little pit stops, if you will—avoiding the need to head back to the nursery every time someone needs changing.

RECOGNIZE POSTPARTUM DEPRESSION

I had postpartum depression, but I didn't realize it at the time. I knew I was depressed, but it seemed like a reasonable response to the situation I was in. It was only when I came out of it that I realized how bad it had been. All my friends told me having kids was a "huge adjustment," but in my case, I felt it went beyond that.

While most women bounce back quickly after childbirth, it's important to note that some women (about 1 in 500) develop postpartum depression (PPD). Although PPD has gotten a lot of press in recent years, there's still a cloud of mystery surrounding it, discouraging many women who may have the condition to seek help. Furthermore, due to the increased hormone production in a multiple pregnancy, new moms with twins are at higher risk for the disorder than moms who've just given birth to singletons.

What Is Postpartum Depression?

Postpartum depression shouldn't be confused with the "baby blues," a common and mild mood disturbance that usually occurs in the first few days following birth. Reports are inconclusive as to whether the baby blues are caused by a rapid postnatal drop in hormones or simply brought on by increased stress and sleep deprivation. Regardless, when a mom has the baby blues, she may find herself upbeat one minute but miserable the next. It doesn't take much to bring her to tears. She's easily agitated, restless, and finds it difficult to concentrate. The condition usually resolves on its own within a week or two postpartum.

Postpartum depression, on the other hand, is caused by chemical changes in the brain. It may start out like the baby blues, but instead of the symptoms slowly dissipating with time, they continue. Depression can be mild, or it can worsen and become severe. Moms with PPD often experience feelings of anxiety, hopelessness, lethargy, changes in appetite (eating too much or too little), and even sleep disturbances. They find themselves unable to cope with the day-to-day responsibilities of family, as intense feelings of isolation and resentment of the babies begin to overcome their lives. Some moms have thoughts of death or even of hurting their babies.

Getting Help for the Blues or Depression

Getting the baby blues immediately following childbirth is perfectly normal (one study suggests 80 percent of all new moms experience some form of it). What with the lack of sleep, hormonal changes, crazy hours, and total disruption to our lives, it's a wonder that we don't just skip town after the birth of our children. Many of the moms that I have interviewed experienced some form of depression in the weeks following the birth of their children. "I let my pride get in the way of asking for help," one mom told me. "If I had been diagnosed by a doctor earlier, things would have gotten sorted out so much quicker."

You can keep the blues to a minimum by giving up housework and instead sleeping more often. To combat the feelings of isolation, get out of the house on a regular basis, whether it's for a neighborhood stroll with the twins or a few hours away without them—allowing you to communicate with the outside world. At the very least, get a bit of sunlight as some research suggests that it can help lessen the feelings of depression. Other studies show that exercising—three times a week for an hour—greatly reduces symptoms of depression, too. And finally, share your feelings with family and friends—reach out to those who care about you.

If your symptoms persist, don't discount them. Seek professional help. (If asking for help is difficult for you, start with a phone call to your obstetrician.) Depression of any kind in postpartum women should never be dismissed or ignored.

Feeding Your Babies

Feed, burp, diaper change. Feed, burp, diaper change. A newborn nurses or drinks a bottle and has his or her diaper changed an average of 10 times a day. Now multiply that by two and you've got one busy life.

BREASTFEEDING

Before I had my twins I told people my plan to breastfeed. People thought I was crazy, that it was impossible. But my mind was set. I was also convinced that it wasn't fair to have a baby wait for a bottle, and breastfeeding them at the same time would solve that and keep them on the same schedule, too. I breastfed for 15 months. It was one of the most important things I've ever done, and the most challenging. I'm really proud of my accomplishment.

Nearly all women are capable of breastfeeding. However, breastfeeding makes much harder demands on the mother of twins than on her mother-of-singleton counterpart, at least during the beginning stages. There's a learning curve associated with breastfeeding—one that's compounded when there are *two* to nurse—that simply doesn't exist with either singleton nursing or even with bottle feeding. It's why so many moms of multiples give it up—far more than moms of singletons. (Although a recent government report finds that nearly 75 percent of new moms with singletons nurse their babies for at least the first few months, the percentage of mothers of multiples, especially those with premature twins, is drastically lower.) Yet once the mother of twins and her babies become comfortable with the arrangement (for first-time moms, it might take a month or more), the opposite is true. Nursing, by far, is much easier than bottle feeding.

Therefore, if you're truly committed to nursing your twins, it's important to educate yourself on how to nurse *before* their arrival, line up a lactation consultant just in case you have problems once you've begun the process, and have some kind of help at home during the first few weeks. If someone else is available to cook meals, do laundry, and keep the house in reasonable order, you'll then be free to concentrate on learning the art of breastfeeding.

Understanding Breast Milk Production

I should have been more insistent in the hospital that they not give formula. I should have been more willing to try to nurse them right after my C-section. I blame myself to some degree because I felt so awful—physically and emotionally—that I didn't want to deal with breastfeeding. I let the nurses tell me it wouldn't matter if I waited until I felt better, but the babies never learned to nurse properly in the hospital. And, once we got home, I was so overwhelmed I just couldn't cope. I needed to recover my own strength and that wasn't possible while nursing two babies around the clock.

Immediately following birth, your body produces colostrum. A forerunner to milk, colostrum is a thin, yellowish fluid rich with infection-fighting antibodies and protein, a great benefit to new babies. But don't be surprised when you see how little colostrum your body produces at a time. (Personally, I was shocked. *That's it?*) No need to panic thinking that you are starving your babies; they are born with enough food and water to survive five days! So don't worry about undernourishment, just spend those first few days concentrating on helping your babies latch on, and pumping to get your milk supply up and going.

After several days of your twins' sucking, your body will produce "mature milk." You'll know that your milk has "come in" (between the second and fifth day after giving birth) when your breasts begin to feel full or engorged due to the increased blood rushing to them and when you hear your babies actually swallowing while they nurse. It's important during this time to nurse frequently to ensure that your body will produce an adequate supply of milk as your milk will gradually increase over the next week. Remember, breastfeeding works on a supply-and-demand basis. The more they demand, the more your body will supply. This is not the time to put your babies on a strict feeding schedule either. Your twins should nurse on demand to guarantee a successful start to your milk production. In addition, nursing mothers need extra nutrition to keep up a healthy milk supply, and while some may be anxious to lose those extra pregnancy pounds, dieting while nursing is not a good idea.

Advantages of Breast Milk

No other food is more perfect for your newborns than your breast milk.

- **Provides complete balance of nutrients.** Breast milk offers the ideal balance of nutrients for the first six months of life (others say it's closer to a year). Not only is breast milk easier for babies to digest than infant formula, it also protects them against infection and allergies. Breastfeeding lessens babies' constipation and colic, and they usually spit up less. Recent studies suggest breastfed babies have slightly higher IQ scores, a lower incidence of sudden infant death syndrome (SIDS), and a lower incidence of obesity later in life.

- **Promotes bonding.** The skin-to-skin contact between mother and baby helps to build a trusting relationship. This is especially important for the mother of multiples, who often has a more difficult time in bonding with two children at once. As soon as the tricks of breastfeeding are learned, most mothers find it pleasurable—a time to nuzzle and love their babies.

- **Offers physical benefits.** Breastfeeding helps the uterus to return to its prepregnancy shape more quickly than that of a woman who isn't breastfeeding. In addition, breastfeeding uses up calories, helping moms to lose weight faster.

- **Saves money.** The average family spends approximately $160 to $200 a month (a whopping $1,920 to $2,400 annually) on infant formula for twins. Breast milk costs nothing.

- **Saves time.** There are no bottles to sterilize, no formula to mix, no waiting while someone warms a bottle. Breast milk is always the proper temperature and never needs refrigeration.

- **Delays menstruation.** A mother who breastfeeds exclusively (no supplemental bottles) and often (and with twins, you will) may delay her period for many months (I held out for 11).

Breastfeeding Twins

Nursing twins poses a challenge for new families, but with a little experimentation, mothers of multiples can enjoy the benefits that nursing offers. To keep milk production plentiful, remember to drink plenty of fluids, eat nutritiously, and nurse frequently. Also, having each baby suck at a breast simultaneously encourages the letdown reflex (the release of milk from the breast) and provides a strong stimulus to the body to produce more milk. Therefore, nursing twins together, at least sometimes, makes good sense. Besides, tandem nursing, as it's called, saves a lot of time over nursing each twin individually. And which mom of twins couldn't use a bit more time?

While it's important for each baby to switch breasts periodically so that each receives proper stimulus from both directions, switching breasts also helps to prevent engorgement if babies have different sucking styles. It's not necessary, however, to switch during a single nursing session as mothers of singletons do. Instead, switch babies daily or at every other session.

Are My Babies Getting Enough?

I tried to breastfeed but for those six weeks, it was mostly about me and the pump and my dwindling supply. If I could have a do-over, I'd take the time necessary for me and the boys to get it worked out ourselves—we were new to the concept—without my hubby and mother hovering nearby ready with a bottle of formula.

Many new moms fear that their new babies aren't getting enough nutrition from nursing and rush to supplement with formula. It's normal to be worried that your twins may not be getting enough milk, but before you consider supplementation, make sure it's necessary by asking yourself these questions.

- Are babies nursing 8 to 12 times daily?

- Do babies nurse for at least 10 minutes each time?

- Do babies have at least six to eight wet diapers daily?

- Are babies having several bowel movements each day?

- Are babies gaining an adequate amount of weight?

- Have babies regained their birth weight by three weeks of age?

Breastfeeding Positions

Both babies are in the cradle position with their legs overlapping.

One baby (left) is in the football hold, while the other is in the cradle position.

Both babies are in the football hold.

If you answered yes to these questions, perhaps your twins' crying means something other than hunger. The need to suck in a baby is very strong during the first year of life, and often an infant cries after being removed from the breast because he or she merely wants to linger a bit longer. Using a pacifier directly after nursing will often satisfy the need to suck and quiet a baby quickly.

But What If They Need Supplementation?

Sometimes a mother has a difficult time producing enough milk. Increasing the number of times she nurses daily along with boosting her fluid consumption is usually enough to augment her milk production and subsequently satisfy her babies. But sometimes due to various health reasons, a woman can't produce enough milk to feed both her babies. In this case, a woman should discuss with her pediatrician the possibility of supplementing nursing with infant formula.

A mother who wants to breastfeed but supplements during the early weeks should proceed with caution—offering a bottle too soon could cause nipple confusion where the baby ultimately chooses the bottle over the breast. In addition, if she offers the bottle too often, her milk supply will decline and she'll be forced to switch to the bottle full-time. A mother should also try to avoid alternating full days with bottle or breast, for that too will cut down on milk production. To make supplementation work, therefore, a mom should offer a complementary bottle after the evening nursing session when her milk supply is at its lowest. If her baby is still hungry, he or she will take it.

Breast Pumps

Sooner or later, a nursing mom will have a need for a breast pump. Some, like me, learned to use a pump while still in the hospital, where between nursing sessions, I pumped my breasts and then gave the expressed colostrum to my newborns. Not only were they getting an extra dose of this important forerunner to milk, but by pumping, I was encouraging my breasts to build up an adequate supply of milk—an important benefit since I wanted to nurse my twins exclusively.

Breast pumps are most useful when a mom must return to work but wants to continue nursing her babies. It also offers a little freedom to new parents by allowing someone else to give babies bottles of expressed milk. A word of caution: Remember that giving your babies bottles too soon can cause nipple confusion. Introduce a bottle slowly (one per week) and only after breastfeeding has been established (after a month or so). If you have questions or concerns, contact a lactation consultant or call La Leche, an international organization dedicated to educating women on the art of breastfeeding.

Most mothers choose to rent electric pumps rather than purchasing one (although I found the handheld manual Avent Isis pump easy to use and very compact). There is also a special attachment that will allow you to pump both breasts at once. Not only does this save time, but pumping your breasts together stimulates the letdown reflex and encourages milk production.

BOTTLE FEEDING

I think that if you're able to nurse your babies, that's wonderful. But if you can't, don't beat yourself up over it.

Whether it's lack of breastfeeding education, problems with infant prematurity, insufficient milk supply, or simply a lifestyle choice, some mothers opt to bottle feed their twins.

TOP FIVE BREASTFEEDING BOO-BOOS

Learning how to breastfeed takes lots of practice and patience on the part of mother and child. Avoid breastfeeding problems before they start by sidestepping these boo-boos.

1. **Not educating yourself on breastfeeding.** While breastfeeding is a natural process, it doesn't come naturally. A woman (and her child) must learn how to breastfeed. Read everything you can on breastfeeding, take a breastfeeding seminar (offered by many local hospitals), or attend a La Leche meeting for help.

2. **Not nursing frequently enough.** Newborns need to nurse every one and a half to three hours. To an exhausted new mom of twins, it may be tempting to stretch the feedings a little further

continued

apart. But it's important to nurse frequently during the first month in order to establish a good supply of milk. If you want to breastfeed exclusively, don't put babies on a schedule until breastfeeding has been fully established.

3. **Not using good positioning.** When you're uncomfortable, fumbling with your baby, you're setting yourself up for an unpleasant experience. Find a cozy spot either on the sofa or in a rocking chair, and take a moment to properly position your baby by placing him or her in a cradle hold (head resting in the crook of your right elbow). With your left hand, support your right breast using the "C" hold (four fingers below your breast, thumb on top). Never push your breast toward your baby. Instead, when the baby's mouth is open, move him or her to your breast. When one baby is done nursing, repeat the process on the other side with the co-twin.

4. **Not waiting patiently for baby to open mouth wide enough.** The secret to breastfeeding success is a proper latch on, but a mom in a hurry often tries to put the baby to her breast before the baby is ready. Cradle baby close and tickle his or her lips with your nipple to encourage the baby to open the mouth wide. Only when the mouth is open wide should you pull your baby in to latch on. Once your baby is on your breast, check to see that the lips are correctly positioned—he or she should be sucking at least a 1-inch radius around the areola. If your twin is sucking just your nipple or if his or her bottom lip is tucked in, detach your baby by slipping your finger inside the mouth to release his or her grip and start the latch-on process over again.

5. **Introducing bottles too soon.** It may be tempting to give your babies bottles of expressed milk or formula during the first month, but it may lead to nipple confusion, where your babies end up favoring the bottle and rejecting your breast in the process. Wait until breastfeeding has been correctly established (between four and six weeks) before offering your babies artificial nipples.

Advantages of Bottle Feeding

While I have felt guilty about not breastfeeding, I know that it was the right choice for our family. My husband was able to be completely involved, and I was able to be away for feedings, if needed. This did wonders as it allowed me to sleep some and to keep my sanity. In the end, I think we have handled the demands of having twins very well. We have great kids! If I had killed myself with breastfeeding I don't think I would have been as good a mother.

- **Anyone can feed the babies.** Bottle feeding helps many new families to better cope with the added stress that newborn twins bring into the household. Anyone from Dad to Grandma to a babysitter can take over at mealtime, giving Mom a much needed break.

- **Dads can take a more active parenting role.** Some husbands report feeling left out while their wives solely take on the job of nursing the children. Bottle feeding allows dads to be more involved by sharing feeding responsibilities with their spouses.

- **Babies can go for longer periods between feedings.** A breastfed newborn usually nurses every one and a half to three hours, while a formula-fed infant averages a bottle every three to four hours.

- **Bottle feeding is easier in public.** Many Americans still find breastfeeding in public to be distasteful, and it's not uncommon to see a nursing mother hiding in a corner or banished to a public restroom trying to nurse her baby. It's much easier to give a hungry baby a bottle at a restaurant or museum.

- **Keeping track of the amount taken is easier.** One of nursing mothers' biggest complaints is not knowing how much their babies have drunk and whether it was enough. With bottles, it's easy to note the amount of formula each baby has consumed.

- **Mom has more time for sleep.** If Mom shares the nighttime feedings with her spouse or another member of the household, she will ultimately get more sleep.

Bottle Feeding Twins

I had such complications after delivery that I was not able to get a good milk supply. After four days, I was so far behind the eight

ball. I was really upset about it. I cried to a nurse who gave me
the best advice—if Mommy's not happy, then babies are not
happy. I felt like she had given me permission not to feel so bad. I
tried but gave up after three weeks. I think the pressure to nurse is
unfair, and I feel resentful that the commercials and
advertisements make mothers like me feel inferior. I love and
nurture my boys as much as the next mother.

If only the mother of twins just had an extra pair of hands, life would
be a bit easier. While it is possible to bottle feed both babies at once,
try to bottle feed one at a time at least once a day by distracting the less
hungry baby with either a toy or pacifier. All newborns crave skin-to-
skin contact with their caregivers, and bottle feeding a single baby
cradled within your arms offers just that. When you do feed both at
once, avoid propping their bottles. Instead, try one of the positions illus-
trated and give each baby lots of eye contact and comforting words.

Nighttime Feedings

Nighttime is the worst time for any new parent. Problems seem magnified tenfold at 4 A.M. The problem is in a scheduling conflict—many
new babies experience "turnaround," where they are awake most of the

Bottle Feeding Positions

One baby sits in a car seat, while the other rests on a pillow directly in front of
his twin.

With babies secured in their car seats, their mom can easily feel both at once.

night and sleep most of the day (much to the disappointment of their moms and dads). Try changing the pattern by stimulating your babies during the day with lots of playtime and an afternoon bath, and then slowly winding things down around dinnertime in preparation for bedtime.

New parents of twins desperately need sleep. But how do they get any when there are two little people waking every few hours demanding to be fed? It took a bit of experimentation, but eventually the parents I spoke with invented all sorts of wonderful nighttime strategies. Whichever method you try, remember to wake both babies at the same time. The benefits are enormous—it saves time and encourages both twins to be on the same schedule, giving you a moment of peace. If you choose to "feed on demand," however, once you feed one twin and head back to bed, just as soon as you fall asleep, his or her co-twin is sure to wake up!

Bottle-Feeding Strategies for Night

We'd take turns being "on duty." The "on duty" parent would be the first one to get up when the first baby woke. That parent would warm the bottles, change the first baby's diaper, and then wake the other parent. The second baby was almost sure to be screaming by this time and then would get her diaper changed. When the bottles were warm, we'd both feed them. Then the "on duty" parent went to bed while the other parent cleaned up and got the bottles ready for the next feeding.

After feeding the babies together in the evening, I would go to bed around 8 or 9 P.M. My husband stayed up and fed them again around 11 P.M. When they woke in the middle of the night, I fed them. Then when they woke in the morning, we both got up to feed them. With this schedule, we were each getting around six hours of sleep each night.

Since my preemie twins were on a three-hour schedule, we took rotating shifts with my parents. While two people slept in beds upstairs, one person would sleep on the couch in the family room (the babies were in a pack-n-play in the dining room). The person on the couch would do the midnight feeding. When he was done, he'd wake someone in a bed who would then go to sleep on the couch until the 3 A.M. feeding. After he was done, he'd wake another person who'd sleep on the couch until the 6 A.M. feeding.

We had friends who came over once every couple of weeks to do an evening feeding; my husband and I would go to bed at 7 P.M. Our friends would do the 10 P.M. feeding and then stay until the babies started to fuss again around midnight. Then they'd wake us just before they left. We could get four to five hours of sleep in a row that way.

Breastfeeding Strategies for Night

When the boys would wake at night, we both got up. While I went to the bathroom and got a glass of water, my husband would start changing diapers. He then helped position both babies on my nursing pillows and went back to bed. When I was done, I'd signal to him to come and help put the babies back in their crib. Other nights, when one baby woke, he'd change his diaper and then bring him to me in bed where I'd snooze and nurse at the same time. That baby would stay with us until the next baby woke. My husband would then trade babies, putting one back in his crib and bringing the other to me. It may not have been the safest having the boys sleep with us and it sure made my husband work, but at least I got to sleep a bit more.

I would scoop up both babies from their crib (if only one was awake, I'd grab the other as well), carefully carry both of them down the hallway to the living room, and then place them in their bouncy seats right in front of the recliner. I would strap on my nursing pillow and then pick up both babies and bring them to my chest as I sat down in the recliner. Then I'd position the babies in the football hold. Once they were pros at latching on, I just had to place my breasts in their vicinity and they would latch on. I would use my arms and elbows to keep their bodies close to me.

TOP FIVE BEDTIME STRATEGIES

When babies are finally tucked away in their cribs for the night, parents of multiples all over the world voice a collective sigh of relief. Unfortunately, some babies won't cooperate at the appointed hour, setting up the rest of the evening for a stressful battle. Here are some ideas to ease the nighttime woes.

1. **Develop a routine.** Doing the same thing at the same time each evening encourages kids to respond by expecting and accepting bedtime. Whether it's bath time, storytime, bedtime, or a bottle in front of the TV and then bedtime, keep the nighttime ritual calm, enjoyable, and consistent.

2. **Allow no naps after 4 P.M.** Often, if children take late afternoon naps, they aren't tired at bedtime. Try having naptime during the morning and midafternoon; then use the early evening for bathing and quiet playtime. Naps shouldn't extend beyond four hours at a clip either.

3. **Cluster feed.** To help babies sleep through the night, try feeding or nursing them every two hours in the afternoon and early evening so they won't be as hungry during the nighttime. But remember, don't offer cereal. Introducing solids before six months in the hopes of having babies sleep through the night may actually disturb their sleep patterns.

continued

4. **Differentiate between night and day.** Keep daytime bright and busy. Don't close the curtains or turn off the radio just because it's naptime. Conversely, don't blare the TV at night. Instead, keep lights dim and turn off the telephone ringer. These tips will help send signals to your babies to associate the daytime for activity and nighttime for quiet.

5. **Support "I want my blankie."** Encourage attachment to transitional objects like a blanket. At bedtime, offer babies their blankets as you guide them into bed. The comfort associated with the item helps children soothe themselves to sleep.

Bathing and Dressing

Bathing newborns is often a stressful event—they don't take well to water. To deal with the situation, many parents choose to bathe their babies only several times a week rather than every day. Yet others find that the bath is a relaxing time for their twins and use the ritual daily to prepare for bedtime. Other parents employ a third alternative—bathe only one baby a day.

During bath time, try using the assembly-line technique, where one parent washes the infant while the other dries and dresses him or her. And while one resourceful mother recruited the aid of her babysitter during bath days, it is possible to bathe babies solo using the kitchen sink.

- Set up two bouncer seats in the kitchen and within your sight.

- Undress both babies (keeping diapers on until you're ready to put babies into the sink), and safely strap Baby A in a bouncer seat wrapped in a warm blanket if it's chilly. Offer a pacifier, a toy, or a bottle.

- Bathe, dry, and dress Baby B, and then move Baby B to the empty bouncer seat. Offer a pacifier, toy, or bottle.

- Repeat process with Baby A.

Whichever method you choose, have all bath paraphernalia ready and organized at the start of bath time (including soap, shampoo, towels, cotton swabs, clean diapers, pajamas/play clothes) so there will be no need to scramble about while holding a cold, wet, screaming baby. (I tell you this from experience.)

As babies get older, they'll begin to enjoy bath time much more (and so will you). At four months, try bathing twins together in the tub. To help support their backs, sit them each in small, square laundry baskets, as described in Chapter 3. You can forgo the baskets when they are able to sit up on their own (about six months). Another time-saver is to simply bathe with your babies. Just be sure to have an extra pair of hands standing by to help the twins out of the tub.

And remember, **never** leave a baby unattended in the tub or kitchen sink. It only takes a few moments for a baby to drown, even in only a few inches of water. If the doorbell rings, ignore it. Don't answer the telephone; instead let the machine get it.

When it comes to clothing your twins, save those matching sailor suits with all the buttons for a special party or photo op; for day-to-day living, stick with something simple. Cotton stretch suits are the only outfits newborns need for the first few months. The terry material and footy bottoms keep babies warm, while the front-snap enclosures make the countless diaper changes a little easier. And stretch suits are easy to launder. Nightgowns with drawstring bottoms are a nighttime alternative. Although the drawstring bottoms make diaper changes a breeze, it is often cumbersome to pull the dresslike nightgown over a newborn's head.

Of Special Concern—Bathing and Dressing Preemies

Even the smallest stretch suit looks huge on a 4-pound preemie. If you don't want to spend the extra money on specially made clothing for your tiny packages, opt for the nightgowns with drawstrings.

Low birth weight and premature babies have a harder time regulating their body temperature. Keep them warm by dressing them in socks and knit hats, and make sure they're covered with a blanket while sitting in their bouncer seats. During bath time, keep the room draft free and promptly dry babies once they are out of the water.

The Fussy Hour—Will You Live Through It?

Fussing (the polite term for *crying*) is normal and should be expected. Most new parents will tell you that dinnertime—from 5 to 7 P.M.—is the most stressful period of the day and should really be called "the witching hour." Even though they've just been fed and changed, some babies still insist on howling. And when you're dealing with crying twins, the stress can sometimes be overwhelming.

Take heart—some babies never fuss. Not mine, nor anyone else's I know, but I've heard such babies are out there. You might take some comfort in knowing that most babies begin to calm down about the third month. Until then, read on.

FIGHTING THE FUSSY FEST

- **Predict and prepare.** If you find that your babies are most fussy just before dinner, maybe an adjustment to your schedule is needed. Perhaps nursing them during this time will help. Or, before your twins hit the wall, take them for a quick walk around the block in the stroller. In other words, don't wait for the wailing to start before you act—it's often too late by then.

- **Discover tools of the trade.** Experiment with different toys to see which your babies find engaging. Try a motorized bouncer seat, soft soothing music, a baby video (my boys liked watching one with fish), a swing, or a double snugly sack.

- **Consider whether to plug or not to plug.** Any parent will tell you that a pacifier isn't called a pacifier for nothing—it works. But many parents worry that a pacifier will ruin young teeth. And who thinks a five-year-old child sucking one is endearing? Not many. Yet, pediatricians say we shouldn't worry. During the first year of life, a baby's need to suck is so strong that many doctors recommend it and parents shouldn't discourage its use.

- **Be inventive.** Moms told me all sorts of tricks they came up with from taking all clothes off of babies and letting them lie on a blanket on the floor ("Babies love to be naked!") to tightly swaddling them and patting their bottoms. And finally, "If they're crying and you've ruled out all the major reasons—hunger, poopy diaper—then it's time to vacuum the floor," one mom explained. "You know your floor needs it anyway, and the noise is loud enough to make the babies notice. I'd park my boys in their bouncy chairs, and they'd watch me vacuum."

Playtime

Infants may not do much, but even very young babies are like sponges, just waiting to absorb any stimuli offered to them. You won't be able to play catch with your one-month-old twins, but they will benefit from any interaction you offer them. The trouble is that with all the diaper changing, feeding, and laundry duty that twins require, there seems to be very little time to give them intimate contact. Start the playtime process by turning everyday tasks like diaper changing into a form of play. Nibble on toes, blow raspberries on stomachs, or just gaze for a moment into their eyes. When your babies begin to "ooh" and "ah" in response to all your tenderness, answer them back. As they get older, provide some simple stimulation as well in the form of large, colorful toys; mobiles; and play gyms.

Bonding with Twins: The Truth Versus the Myths

Some new parents feel an instant connection to their babies. From the moment they see each other, it's love at first sight. But for others, the bond between parent and child takes more time. If complications such as an emergency cesarean arise during delivery, for instance, or if babies are born prematurely and are whisked off to the neonatal intensive care unit (NICU), a parent's prenatal fantasy of a joyful first meeting could be postponed, further complicating the bonding process.

If you don't feel instant sparks, rest assured that the feeling of parental love will ultimately prevail. Just remember that the parent-child attachment is a process and comes in all forms, with everyone working on his or her own time schedule.

For many of the moms that I interviewed, bonding with their twins came slowly and evolved over the course of weeks, even months, as the realization of motherhood gradually sank in. "I don't know how much of it was postpartum depression or how much was just having twins, but I didn't feel like I bonded with them until almost four to five months," said one mom. "I was fond of them, as if I were their babysitter. I thought they were cute, and I wanted them to be healthy and happy. But I never felt that instant, overwhelming love many mothers talk about. That has grown gradually and gets stronger every day."

The majority of moms simply found it hard to find the time to bond. "From birth they've done everything at the same time—eating, sleeping, pooping," explained another mom. "I feel like I'm constantly just meeting their needs. It never feels like there is enough time in the day to actually spend quality time with just one of them or teach them things. I don't know if I'll ever be able to get a good balance."

Unlike animals, who are able to bond with a group of young all at the same time, humans can bond with only one offspring at a time. For parents of multiples, this can present a temporary problem as they try to bond individually with each of their twins. Twins, especially identical, look so much alike at birth that it's often difficult for mothers and fathers to separate them. It's much easier for parents, therefore, to bond with the twins together as a unit. Unit bonding eventually gives way to individual bonding as parents begin to notice the differences in their children.

Hospital-bound preemies pose a challenge to new parents as well. It's not uncommon for a recuperating mom bound to the house to fall in love with the first-home twin while the dad (usually the appointed liaison between hospital and home) feels closer to the twin still recovering in the NICU. In fact, an Australian study revealed that when twins left the hospital at different intervals, they were perceived differently by their mothers, with the twin leaving first being viewed as more favorable. Furthermore, the longer the other baby stayed behind, the more negatively the mother rated that twin's behavior regardless of how well he or she was progressing.

Other parents report feeling closer to the more responsive twin, or the twin who is easier or less fussy. "One of my boys screamed for about 16 hours a day, so I really struggled to bond with him," one mom remembered. "Funny, now he's probably the most affectionate and connected of all my children."

When a parent admits to feeling closer to one twin, it helps to lessen the guilt often associated with it. Parents need time to feel connected to both babies, and it's perfectly natural for one twin to appeal to one parent more than another. In time, the feelings for one child will flip-flop to the other child and then flip-flop again.

TECHNIQUES TO PROMOTE BONDING

The idea of infant massage came out of guilt when breastfeeding didn't work out. I did piles of research and came to the conclusion that the act of breastfeeding—the physical closeness, the skin-to-skin contact—is as important as the actual breast milk. We decided that although we were giving them a bottle, we would do as much of the other stuff associated with breastfeeding as possible. We found it a great way to connect and bond with our babies one-on-one for five minutes a day in an otherwise chaotic time.

Feelings of closeness can't be manufactured or rushed. And although bonding takes time as parents get to know the new kids on the block, nature can be helped along.

During Pregnancy

Ultrasound photos can distinguish the position of each baby, helping moms and dads to recognize distinct traits in utero. Once I learned the positions of my sons, I couldn't help but notice how often Michael got hiccups, yet that annoying little habit actually helped to endear him to me. (He still gets them often to this day.)

In the Hospital

Parents should try to hold their babies as soon as possible following the birth. If Mom is too weary or drugged from delivery, Dad should step in and begin the process. Having babies room in with their mothers instead of spending time in the hospital nursery allows parents 24-hour access to their twins as well. The skin-to-skin contact of breastfeeding also fosters the relationship between mother and child. And if babies are born prematurely, requiring a lengthy stay in the NICU, parents should visit often and hold their twins as much as the staff will allow. Speak to your doctor about having them come home together rather than separately.

At Home

I just tried to make each of them laugh. Different things would spark their laughter; then when one was laughing, the other would follow suit. If you can make a child laugh, you don't have to worry about the connection, it's already there.

Once new parents arrive at home with their twins, the real bonding begins. Study each baby individually, looking for differences in appearance and personality. Respond to the needs of each baby separately. And use his or her name frequently. Spend time alone (even if it's just a few minutes) with each baby at some point during the day. And make sure you alternate babies with your partner—from diaper changes to bottle feeding, get equal access with each twin.

Top Five Ways for Fathers to Bond with Twins

With so much emphasis on the mother-child relationship, fathers sometimes get overlooked. Moms have a distinct bonding advantage over dads—women carry children for nine months and are able to breastfeed. Yet men can establish strong relationships with their twins early on by focusing their attention on getting to know their babies and following these tips.

1. **Know the drill.** While mothers generally rule the roost when it comes to issues of child rearing, fathers don't have to take a backseat role. Get to know your twins' schedule—when do they go down for naps? When do they get fed? Then jump in with assistance without being asked.

2. **Watch your timing.** Take time off from work immediately following the delivery by using vacation time or taking advantage of the Family and Medical Leave Act.

3. **Play rub-a-dub-dub.** Many dads find that the nightly ritual of giving their babies a bath is a pleasant and special way to connect with their children.

4. **Allow Mom a day alone.** Whether it's a stroll through the park or a trip to the hardware store or supermarket, take the babies out for the day. Not only will your wife appreciate the time alone, but you'll develop an even greater appreciation for her job as primary caregiver.

5. **Join or start a daddy-and-me play group.** More than ever, fathers are taking an active role in their children's lives. Why not take it a step further and start a play group specifically for dads and their kids? Once a month, organize a play date at a local park, invite friends and colleagues with kids, and do what women have been doing for years—share parenting tips, offer emotional support, and just have fun.

Four Weeks and Counting

During that first month with your newborn twins, you are sure to experience a wide range of emotions, from total elation at what remarkable little beings you have created to sheer bewilderment. This emotional roller-coaster ride is not only natural, it should be expected. While this period can be extremely exhausting, it will pass. And though it may be hard to imagine now, there will come a time when you will look back nostalgically and wish for those early days again.

ₒ5ₒ

Months 2 Through 6

Unless you've gone through it, you simply don't get it. I was in a fraternity in college and they kept us up for five days straight. This is similar to that, but three months long. Then, you get some sleep and you realize that the person that you've been, isn't who you are. That first night when both kids slept for eight hours, my wife woke up singing "A Spoonful of Sugar," and I was whistling "Zip-A-Dee-Doo-Dah." And we were both like, "I remember how fun we are!"

Who would have ever thought that four weeks would go by so slowly? But now that you've mastered the art of infant burping, you feel like an old pro ready to offer advice to other expectant parents. Yes, the worst is over—but a whole new set of problems has cropped up, like how will you ever manage twins now that you're home alone? And how does one person get out of the house with two babies?

Developmental Milestones

By the second month, your babies have grown more accustomed to their surroundings. They sleep less and spend more time alert and awake (that is, if someone interacts with them). Their newborn jerky movements have also subsided as they have begun to voluntarily manipulate their own bodies. As muscle tone improves, you'll marvel at all their kicking and squirming as they exercise their bodies. Their eyesight has improved, too. Your twins can focus up to 12 inches away. Watch as they follow an object or person across the room. They also take immense pleasure in staring at their hands for long periods of time and mouthing their fists. Your twins may look alike, but strong differences in personalities begin to unfold. For instance, one may be an early bird, asleep before eight in the evening and up with the sun, while the other thrives as a night owl, refusing to close his eyes until well past 9 P.M.

During the second month your twins will discover their own voices and begin to vocalize, often to each other, as they lie together in their crib. They love to listen to you, just as much as they enjoy listening to their own sounds, so be sure to give them plenty of verbal stimuli by talking and singing to them.

Look for more control of neck muscles in the beginning of the third month. Not only can the twins turn their heads from side to side, but when put on their stomachs they can lift their heads off the floor for a few seconds. You'll also see something you've been waiting a long time for—a smile. It's a big payback for all those sleepless nights. And speaking of sleep, depending on their weight, your babies may begin to sleep through the night (a five- or six-hour stretch, anyway). As they interact with you more, you'll notice that their crying has diminished, too. They still won't interact with each other, but they will focus on each other for a few moments at a time, and, on occasion, one twin may even reach to touch his or her sibling's hand. Although it might not seem like it, on some level, each knows that the other is there, and they often prove it by sleeping nestled together or by sucking on the other's fingers or toes. Perhaps they think their twin is merely an extension of themselves.

The fourth month is an important one. Your twins are no longer newborns—they have graduated to babyhood! By now they can move their heads in all directions and lift them to a 90-degree angle when lying on their stomachs. Their world is now in color, too, as their eyes are able to focus at different distances. Hand-eye coordination has improved as well. You'll notice this as they spy an object, grab it, and slowly bring it to their mouths for a taste. Now's the time to remove your dangling jewelry, away from their reach and powerful grasp. Socially, your twins are developing a sense of humor and will giggle and laugh when tickled. Now babies require lots of stimuli to keep them from getting bored and fussy.

By the fifth month, it's time to think about babyproofing as your little guys start to roll and use this new trick to get into all sorts of trouble. They can probably sit up with a little support and love to take an upright stroll outdoors. Their speech is taking on new sounds, too. Lots of grunts and groans, tongue clicking, raspberries, and even pretend coughing. Listen carefully for the sound *da-da* as they learn to put vowels and consonants together. Encourage their language development by talking to them regularly, telling them the names of new objects.

It's the twins' half birthday by the sixth month, and already they're moving in opposite directions. A new mode of transportation, crawling, usually appears in the sixth month. Whether they choose to creep with their stomachs dragging along the floor or simply wait a month and dive right in with a traditional crawl, you'll marvel at how fast they can scoot across the room. Don't worry if one baby is more mobile than the other. It's inevitable that your twins will show significant differences in coordination. All babies fluctuate in skill level, and twins are no exception. At this stage, some babies focus on physical and motor skills like rolling and crawling, while others prefer to explore their social skills like vocalizing and interacting with the family. Before long, the lagger will catch up and maybe even pass his or her twin in skills.

If you haven't already done so, it's time for babies to part company and sleep in separate cribs. By month six, most babies are too big and too restless to share the same crib, but no need to put them in separate rooms—twins sleep better as roommates.

Home Alone

The in-laws have returned to New Jersey, the frozen dinners are all gone, and your spouse has just left to return to work full-time. This is the first day that you're alone with the kids. As you gaze at the two little cherubs snoozing soundly in their bouncer seats, fear takes over. "What will I do if they both wake up at once?" you wonder. "And what if they both start to cry?" Glad you asked.

TROUBLESHOOTING

I told myself I could do it alone—I have two hands. With a lot of propping and Boppy pillows I got myself through it, and within days I was a pro. When they were small infants, I'd do my best to get out of the house. I would drive down to the local drive-thru coffee place, get a coffee, and read in the car while I would let my babies nap. It gave me practice getting out of the house, a change of atmosphere, and a chance to see other people. As I got more comfortable and confident, I moved on to other places like the grocery store or mall. Getting out is worth the effort—it gives back some normalcy.

One parent plus two babies equals not enough hands. I asked parents, "What was the hardest part about being alone with your new babies?" Overwhelmingly, new parents responded that the three hardest parts were when both twins cry at once, putting both down for a nap at the same time, and getting out of the house with both in tow. Many invented tricks for dealing with the pressure; others just managed to get through it (and now laugh about it). Lucky you—you get to learn from their triumphs and tragedies.

What Do You Do When Both Cry at Once?

For some parents, it didn't happen often. For others, it happened every day. To the first-time mom or dad, it can be very stressful when both babies cry at the same time.. By the way, several parents recommended reading the book or watching the video *The Happiest Baby on the Block*, by Harvey Karp, whose triple-whammy of swaddling, pacifier, vigorous movement while "shushing" in a crying baby's ear seems to work wonders.

- **Don't panic.** Although their clenched fists, red faces, and high-pitched screams may seem like they're about to explode, their crying hurts you more than it hurts them. First, quickly assess the situation—is anyone injured? Are they hungry? Do they need changing? Are they too cold? Too hot? If not, then it's time to dig into your bag of tricks and start performing.

- **Become doubly mobile.** If singing or gently talking to your crying twins doesn't do the trick, strap them into their car seats/infant carriers and move them around the house. Usually a change of scenery is all they need to calm down. (I'd sit my boys in their bouncy seats on the front porch where they could watch birds, trees swaying in the breeze, and even the occasional neighborhood cat who would stop by.) Even on cold days, if babies are dressed properly, the outdoors is a great relaxer. If the stroller is handy, go for a walk around the block.

- **Pack 'em up.** Try putting one in a front snuggly and the other in a backpack or even a stroller and move around either indoors or outside. Some babies like to be on the move, sitting still is just not for them.

- **Take care of the squeaky wheel.** Place the less fussy baby in a safe spot (like inside a crib or playpen) with a musical toy, and then attend to the more out-of-control baby.

- **Grab their attention.** Turn on music . . . loudly. Run the vacuum. Put a movie on the home theater system. Anything to quickly get their attention.

How Do You Put Them Both to Sleep?

Rather than placing fussy babies directly into their cribs, many parents working solo just let their twins fall asleep in their car seats/infant carriers or in their vibrating bouncy seats (I know I did). It's safe, comfortable for babies, and allows Mom or Dad to move the sleeping infants anywhere in the house. Other parents strap one baby in a motorized swing and then walk the floor with the second baby nestled in a snugly sack or sling. If you bottle feed your babies, many moms put their babies in Boppy pillows and move them close together so they can feed simultaneously. Once babies have drifted off, the parents then move each baby to a crib or just let him or her snooze on the Boppy pillow.

If you breastfeed your twins to sleep, putting both to bed by yourself is a little trickier, especially if you nurse them together. Some moms have no problem maneuvering two swaddled bundles onto a breastfeeding pillow, but it takes practice. When I was alone, I would often nurse one baby at a time. Whoever was fussier got to go first while the calmer baby patiently waited for a turn nearby, content to suck on a pacifier. Other times I would tandem nurse while sitting on the couch. As each baby fell asleep, I'd slowly maneuver that twin off the pillow and onto the couch. From there, it was easier to pick each baby up and place him in the crib.

How Do You Get out of the House with Both?

Make no mistake—going out alone with twins during the first year can be difficult, especially in the beginning when everyone is getting used to a new way of life. Many moms said that during the first few months they relied on family members coming by to lend a hand in getting everyone out of the house. When no one was available, they simply didn't go out. But staying home for long periods of time can be very isolating for new parents. One family, who lived in an upstairs apartment without an elevator and no ground-floor storage for a stroller, had the hardest time. When the mom stayed home alone with her twins, she would put her girls in their crib, lock the apartment door, and carry the stroller downstairs. Then she quickly headed back to get her twins. It made her very nervous, but she knew her girls were safe in their crib.

With no outside help, other moms persevered. "I'm a big believer in sucking it up!" a mom told me. "The first time I took the girls out was actually the day after we got home from the hospital. It was my husband's graduation from the police academy, and I wasn't going to let two babies stop me." Another mom agreed. "I still had many of the same chores and errands after the twins as I had before the twins," she explained. "So I went out to do them, only now I had two infants with me!"

So how should you go about getting out of the house? Build up your confidence and baby savvy by planning short, simple trips to the park or supermarket (leave lengthy sojourns to the beach or museum for the weekends when another adult is available to lighten the load). Be flexible with babies' schedule. Infants sleep easily when there is lots of noise, and they love the gentle movement of a car or stroller, so there's no need to be concerned that they'll miss a nap. Have your refrigerator stocked with bottles of formula or breast milk so you can grab and go. Always restock your diaper bag every evening with an extra change of clothing (a clean shirt for you, too), plenty of diapers and wipes, and pacifiers and rattles, so you can exit your house quickly once your babies are fed and changed (if you dawdle you'll end up having to feed and change them again).

And for urban dwellers who need to use public transportation while toting two tots—many moms left the stroller at home and used snugly sacks instead. The Sleepy Wrap Baby Carrier, a sling made of durable stretch fabric, can comfortably and safely accommodate two infants up to three months old. After that, parents put one baby in a front snugly and the other in a baby backpack.

Going to the Grocery Store

Don't be intimidated to take your twins to the grocery store on your own. You can shop with two babies just as easily as you can with one—it just takes longer. In addition, getting out with your babies is a good way to teach them about their world. Rule number one: Take your time and never go grocery shopping if you're in a hurry. There's no such thing as a quick trip to the market. If you rush, not only will you return home frazzled, vowing never to do it again, but someone could get hurt in the parking lot or in the store. And in the midst of your whirlwind journey, you're bound to forget half of what's on your grocery list.

Seat Assignments

"So where do you put the babies and all the groceries?" you ask. Ah, if only more supermarkets had double shopping carts!

- **One-cart method.** Place one baby securely fastened in a car seat/ infant carrier in the upper portion of the shopping cart (many supermarkets now have infant seats attached to their store carts), and use a snugly sack or sling for the other baby. Food items go in the main compartment of the cart.

- **Two-cart method.** If a snugly sack or sling is a strain on your back, leave both babies in their car seats/infant carriers and use two carts. Pulling one cart while pushing another takes some practice, but with a few trips, you'll be as agile as a circus acrobat. Honestly, it sounds much harder than it is. I did it for years. Granted, I got lots of funny looks, but it did the trick.

After babies reach six months and can sit in the carts unaided, continue to use the two-cart method, but be sure to find carts with seat belts to prevent babies from climbing out. If your store doesn't provide carts with belts, many baby product catalogs feature portable seat belts that work just as well. Luckily many stores now offer double seats in front.

Top Five Ways to Deal with Excessive Public Attention

Twins draw everyone's attention. Their uniqueness crosses all gender, ethnic, and age lines. In the months following the birth, most parents welcome the attention that strangers shower upon their twins, but eventually the novelty wears off. And when the one hundredth person quips, "Hey, double trouble," right when both children are crying uncontrollably, many parents do all they can just to be polite. When too much attention is just too much, try these tips to get away gracefully.

1. **See no evil, hear no evil.** Pretend not to hear a stranger's comment or question, or when you catch an inquisitive look in the corner of your eye, change direction and avoid the encounter.

2. **Let brevity speak volumes.** Keep answers to strangers' questions short and to the point. When someone asks, "Are they twins?" simply smile, say yes, and keep walking.

3. **Go incognito.** By carrying one baby in a sling or snugly sack and pushing the other in a stroller, most people won't even realize they're twins.

4. **Travel in a pack.** Go shopping with a friend and spread the kids around.

5. **Dress twins differently.** Dressing your babies in very different outfits can sometimes throw your adoring public off the scent.

Top Five Quick Comebacks to Annoying Questions and Comments

· ·

Even a well-intentioned stranger sometimes puts a foot in the mouth by asking personal questions or making tiresome comments. If you're feeling exceptionally naughty, give these comebacks a try.

1. **Comment:** "Twins? I'm sure glad they're yours and not mine!"
   Comeback: "Me, too!"

2. **Question:** "Twins? How do you tell them apart?"
   Answer: "I look."

3. **Question:** "Twins? Did you have to use fertility drugs?"
   Answer: "Yes. We hired a shaman to bless us while we made love."

4. **Question:** "Twins? God bless you!"
   Answer: "He did. Twice."

5. **Question:** "Are they twins?"
   Answer: "No. He's an only child. Who's your eye doctor?"

· ·

"The first day that the twins were strong enough to sit up in a double grocery cart, I cried tears of joy," laughed one mom. "I cried all the way into the store. I knew life from that day forward would be easier. It was a good day indeed!"

A word of caution: Never leave children unattended in your car while you search for a spare grocery cart. I often drove around the parking lot several minutes before I found a cart next to a vacant parking space. It took longer, but it gave me peace of mind to have my children with me at all times.

PUTTING BABIES ON A SCHEDULE

Some parents cringe when they think of putting their babies on a schedule. Images of a drill sergeant with a stopwatch and whistle standing over the nursery crib come to mind, and they immediately cry, "Scheduling? Too restrictive! Never!" And in some cases, they're right. Some parents do go overboard in insisting their infants adhere to a rigid agenda. But many parents of multiples feel that scheduling is a must to keep order during chaotic times. And for the full-time, stay-at-home parent with no outside help, it's a question of survival—put the kids on a schedule or perish.

What exactly is scheduling, anyway? Simply put, scheduling means developing a routine—doing the same thing (like feeding, putting them down for a nap, and getting them ready for bed) at the same time every day. Actually, your babies have probably been putting you on a schedule, but you just didn't realize it. After all, they naturally wake up around 6 A.M.; nap around 9 A.M., noon, and 3 P.M.; and then wind down for the day roughly at 8 P.M. The secret now is to take it one step further and slowly fine-tune their routine to better suit your household. Predictability may seem stifling for some, but parents of multiples say it helps everyone in the family function normally.

Benefits of Scheduling

Scheduling is very important for any parent of twins as it keeps your sanity and makes life easier. Start as soon as the babies are in your hands. Feed them together, put them down together, wake them together, change them one after the other.

- **Schedules give structure to daily life.** Knowing what you will be doing at certain times of the day or week gives new parents confidence and a sense of control over their lives, something they often long for after having twins.

- **Babies respond well.** Children crave structure in their lives. With a set routine your babies will grow to expect certain events to happen at certain times of the day, making stressful situations like bedtime much easier.

- **Schedules are twin friendly.** By encouraging both babies to be on the same schedule, parents of multiples can actually find a little one-on-one time to be with each other. Just imagine what life would be like if Baby A napped at 9 A.M., noon, and 3 P.M., while Baby B napped at 11 A.M., 2 P.M., and 5 P.M.—you'd never get a moment to yourself. As one double-duty mom explained, "Scheduling helps you catch up and catch your breath."

Disadvantages of Scheduling

- **Too rigid.** If one baby starts crying at 5 P.M., parents shouldn't look at the clock and say, "How can you be hungry? You're not scheduled to eat for another hour!" A schedule should not be set in stone but used as a guide. Parents must be sensitive to their infants. If your baby cries, it usually means he or she is hungry and should be fed. When a baby cries, he or she is not trying to manipulate—the infant wants something like food, a clean diaper, or just a little attention. These needs should never go unmet.

- **Less mobility.** As your twins get older and refuse to nap in the stroller or car, a schedule often interferes with going out. It's frustrating trying to quickly run errands and get home in time for the afternoon nap when you're concerned about the schedule.

- **Too controlling.** Some parents are so driven by their children's schedule that they put their own lives on hold such as refusing to attend a family function just because it conflicts with naptime.

Tips for Developing a Schedule

- **Adjust slowly.** Realize that during the first few months everyone is adjusting to a new life, and if you push your one-month-old twins to adhere to a rigid schedule, you'll just end up making everyone miserable.

- **Let your babies guide you.** Listen and recognize your babies' cues and then work with them. If Baby A wants to nurse at 6 P.M., encourage Baby B to nurse at that time, too. If Baby B naturally falls asleep around 9 P.M., but you'd prefer her to go to bed with her sister at

TOP FIVE WAYS TO GIVE EACH TWIN
INDIVIDUALIZED ATTENTION

Finding time to give each twin one-on-one attention is a big concern for parents of multiples—especially if your twins are on a schedule and do just about everything together. But even just five minutes a day with one child can be special. Here's how to eke out a few precious moments during your busy day.

1. **Take your time diapering.** It may seem like an odd way to spend quality time with your baby, but during the diapering process, a parent and child often gaze deeply into each other's eyes, making a profound connection.

2. **Nap with one baby.** Not only is napping with your baby a good way to catch up on your sleep, but there's nothing more comforting than the touch of a baby's soft, warm skin and the feel of his or her breath against your cheek. Or do what this mom did: "When they slept, I would pick one up at a time and hold him in my arms. He looked so innocent, like an angel. That's how I was able to connect with each of them."

3. **Nurse or bottle feed just one baby at a time.** Although it saves lots of time to nurse or bottle feed both babies at once, try to feed them separately at least once a day. "I always took advantage of someone coming to help me because I could bond while feeding one baby at a time," a mom added.

4. **Take advantage of the early riser.** If one baby wakes from a nap sooner than expected, quickly whisk that twin out of the nursery before the sibling awakes. Then snuggle on the couch for a while. If one is an early riser, awake with the sun, bring that twin into bed for some family bonding.

5. **Share weekend assignments.** On weekends or whenever another parent is available, let each be responsible for one baby. Take one to the market or sit out in the garden together. During the following weekend, switch babies.

8 P.M., slowly move Baby B's bedtime a few minutes every night until it matches her sister's.

- **Be flexible.** Babies are not robots. As they grow and change, so should their schedule. Things like vacation and air travel, illness, and teething can all throw your babies (and their schedules) off. During these temporary setbacks, let your babies control when they want to eat and sleep. Once the crisis has passed, ease them back into their routine.

SUPPORT GROUPS AND PLAY GROUPS

For those parents who have chosen to stay home to raise their children full-time, the feelings of loneliness and isolation leave many to wonder if it's truly worth it. Local clubs for parents of multiples offer moms and dads a chance to meet other parents in the same position (see the Appendix for addresses of National Organization of Mothers of Twins Clubs both in the United States and around the world). They offer support, valuable information in online forums, and family outings where your twins get a chance to make friends with other twins. It's a good idea to join a club before you give birth, allowing you to get practical tips on dealing with multiples before they arrive. In addition, many clubs sponsor annual clothing exchanges where you can either buy or swap baby apparel, nursery items, and toys (a big money-saver). Most clubs let you audit several meetings before deciding if it's for you. If your area doesn't have a twins' club, form one of your own. Most national chapters not only encourage this but will help you get started.

Participating in a play group is another alternative for homebound parents looking for support. Once a week, a group of parents gather in a local park or someone's home to share lunch and conversation while their children play together. Growing in popularity, play groups are found just about everywhere—through churches, childbirth classes, and twin clubs. It's easy to start your own, too—just meet another stay-at-home parent and her children every week. Then you can seek out new recruits through word of mouth.

A third, but more costly, alternative is to attend a mommy-and-me class offered through places like Gymboree and local YMCAs. Many of these classes have a 50 percent discount for a second child, but some require an additional adult to participate in the class.

Traveling Overnight with the Twins

Sooner or later, we all have to travel overnight with our kids. Adventurous parents—those who believe having kids shouldn't tie a family down—decide to hit the road sooner than the rest of us. The secret to a successful trip with multiples, these parents say, isn't luck or babies' temperaments (although both help), but careful planning, a sense of humor, and a really big car for all the extra paraphernalia.

Create a getting ready to-do list using a computer spreadsheet that you can print up with each new trip. Check off each task you accomplish. Create two categories: Things to pack (diapers, bibs, pacifiers, and medicine) and what needs to be done before leaving (cancel paper and mail, empty kitchen trash, and unplug computers). It will take several tries to fine-tune your list, and updating it after every trip is always helpful.

TRAVELING BY CAR

The best way to initiate the kids to a life of traveling is to take a road trip. All children weighing less than 40 pounds must be restrained in a car seat that meets federal safety standards (those who weigh between 40 and 80 pounds still need a booster seat). If your babies are still in rear-facing seats when you hit the road, be sure to attach sunshades to protect their eyes. Pack a small cooler with snacks, drinks, and baby bottles to keep inside the car (don't forget a trash bag and paper towels for messes). Stop for a stretch and "diaper break" every two hours even if you don't feel like it—use it as a time to check up on your babies. And while it may be tempting to pack everything that your twins will need, remember you can always buy extra diapers on the road. Why stuff the trunk?

Equipment Checklist for Road Warriors

- **Port-a-crib and hook-on chairs.** Both fold up and store easily in your trunk. If your twins are younger than six months, they can easily share one port-a-crib, but you'll need two hook-on chairs. If you visit the in-laws often, one mom recommended buying doubles of both hook-on chairs (or high chairs) and port-a-cribs (she perused second-hand stores and garage sales for cheap, used ones) to keep at your relatives' homes. This way you don't have to tow extra baby equipment on every vacation.

If your trip includes a hotel stay, save on trunk space and leave the port-a-cribs at home. Instead, call the hotel in advance to reserve two cribs. Most hotels offer this service for a nominal fee (always ask when making your reservations). Hotel cribs are small, so you'll need two regardless of your twins' ages. And always call restaurants ahead of time and ask if they have high chairs, otherwise you'll have to schlep your clip-on chairs with you.

- **Separate bags.** Categorize clothes, underwear, and travel paperwork in large, resealable plastic bags and squeeze the extra air out of them before packing in your suitcase. Make it even easier on yourself and pack individual baby outfits in separate bags. If baby needs a change on the road, that bag is much easier to locate and grab without disturbing the contents of the suitcase.

- **Night-light.** An unfamiliar dark room at 2 A.M. spells disaster if you need to get up to attend to your babies.

- **Entertainment.** A set of never-before-seen toys helps to calm the whining. But before you head to the toy store to stock up, little babies are fascinated with anything new so your arsenal can include something as simple as the measuring spoons from the kitchen drawer (my boys loved to chew on them). But dole out the goodies slowly—only one new toy or object at a time. As they get older, a portable DVD player and a plethora of animated Disney movies works magic. One problem—parents in the front seat have to whisper so as not to drown out the dialogue for the kids in back. Solution? Earphones for the kids.

  Eventually, however, you may want to try podcasts, free downloadable radio programs that you can burn onto CDs and play in the car. With a family-oriented podcast, the whole family can enjoy the same entertainment plus it opens up a lively dialogue between parents and kids. Thousands abound on the Internet (go to the podcast section on iTunes for a list of categories from "Kids and Family" to "Science"). My kids are older and enjoy NPR's *Car Talk* and the news quiz, *Wait, Wait, Don't Tell Me,* but little ones are bound to be mesmerized (at least for a 20-minute stretch) by children's stories read aloud.

TRAVELING BY PLANE

When I flew alone with my sons for the first time, I helped myself tremendously by booking three seats, one for each of us (many airlines offer discounts for children under age two). Although the airlines would have allowed me to hold one baby on my lap, I decided against it for the sake of safety as well as my sanity. In addition to the potential risk of holding a baby during a flight, I wouldn't have been able to attend to my other twin if he had needed me. Safety aside, one double-duty mother and father upon returning from England explained the imposition of holding both babies during a flight, "You can't eat or take a sip of coffee because each of you has a baby on your lap. You can't do anything!"

By law, everything in an aircraft must be restrained, yet babies are the exception. Although several organizations are lobbying Congress to make infant restraints mandatory on all airline flights, it's still legal for an adult to hold a child under the age of two on the lap. Fortunately, new products are now coming on the market to help protect lap babies, including Baby B'Air (babybair.com), a flight vest that secures your baby to your lap belt.

If you're planning on taking a flight with your twins, keep in mind that if you don't book seats for them, you will need to be traveling with two adults—airlines prohibit one person from holding two babies. (But who'd want to?) Furthermore, due to the limited number of oxygen masks in each row of seats, the family may have to split up. And while the bulkhead seats offer much more leg room, great for a small play area for the kids once the plane is airborne, you'll have to stow your carry-on bags overhead—not always convenient when you need to quickly grab a diaper or bottle.

Other Tips to Avoid Turbulence in the Sky

- **Call the airline.** Some airlines offer additional help for families with children by providing on-board cribs that fasten to the bulkhead seats and kids' meals on international flights. All airlines require that you bring your own car seats, and some will allow only one car seat per aisle, so be sure to ask.

- **Purchase a portable luggage cart.** Securing your infant car seats on a luggage cart makes navigating through the airport easier. When your babies get older, check your car seats with your luggage and instead use safety restraints designed specifically for young children such as CARES (kidsflysafe.com).

- **Allow extra time.** If your kids don't slow you down, the countless bags, strollers, and car seats will. Leave yourself plenty of extra time to get to your departure gate.

- **Plan for the worst.** Stuck at the Dallas airport at 2 A.M., a friend once roamed the terminal frantically searching for diapers. She never thought that her flight would be delayed for so long and didn't pack enough disposables. Always pack twice as many diapers, bottles, and snacks as you think you'll need.

- **Travel off-peak hours.** If you plan on holding your twins during the flight, travel during off-peak times (midweek is best) to increase your chances of finding additional empty seats. Furthermore, book the aisle and window seats, leaving the middle seat unoccupied. Airlines often won't assign the odd middle seat unless the flight is full.

Europe and Beyond

If you've set your sights on traveling across the ocean, consider these tips.

- **Use ID bracelets/necklaces.** On the off-chance that your children get lost in a crowded museum or park, have your kids wear ID bracelets or necklaces. On the front write the child's name and the statement "Please take me to the American Embassy or the hotel listed on the back." Tape the hotel address to the back, and as you move from city to city, remember to change the hotel address.

- **Consider harnesses.** It may seem like a barbaric way to keep tabs on your kids, but a harness and leash is a safe way to control two energetic toddlers in a crowded airport or train station.

- **Bring umbrella strollers with clips and backpacks.** Some parts of Europe, such as historic city centers and older monuments, aren't stroller-friendly. One double-duty couple recently back from a trip to Great Britain wished they had brought along baby backpacks. "We had forgotten that many of the historic buildings don't have elevators or ramps. One of us always had to stay outside with the kids while the other ran inside to take a look."

Two umbrella strollers with stroller clips and two baby backpacks offer a variety of combinations to suit virtually every touring need: two single strollers; one double stroller (clip the two singles together); one stroller and one backpack; two backpacks.

Getting Out Without the Twins

With all the extra attention that new twins demand, it's no wonder the marriage is often put on hold. But the bond between committed partners should be the more important one—without a cohesive relationship, the family unit could be in jeopardy. To keep your marriage on track, maintain open lines of communication, and most important, insist on time alone as a couple. Every new mom is nervous about leaving her babies for the first time, but you need to force yourselves to get out alone within a few months of the babies' birth. Even if it's just dinner at a local restaurant and a stroll through town, the time away with just your partner is important.

Parents don't necessarily have to leave the house, however, to spend quality time together. Some innovative couples make a date for the backyard patio (after the kids are asleep, of course). A little wine, some candlelight, a frozen dinner (who has time to cook?), and the baby monitor set the mood for intimate conversation and help to respark spousal love.

FINDING A BABYSITTER

If you're lucky enough to have doting grandparents, aunts, or uncles all eager to babysit, you can skip this part. If you're not so fortunate, read on.

These days, babysitting is no longer a dollar-an-hour proposition like it was when I was a teen. While the going rate is about $10 an hour, some seasoned professionals charge up to $15 an hour. Dinner, a movie, and a sitter can set you back nearly $150, so plan your dates carefully.

Many parents are understandably reluctant to leave their young infants with a sitter, but for the sake of sanity as well as the relationship, they need to get over the fear, hire a babysitter, and go out for the evening. If you're hesitant about leaving your twins, ask a trusted friend to

TOP FIVE WAYS TO RENEW MARITAL INTIMACY

Most couples will admit (in private anyway) that when a new baby arrives (let alone two), lovemaking goes out the window. But there are many ways to make your spouse feel loved and needed until that old magic feeling returns.

1. **Focus on being nice.** When the twins won't go to sleep at the appointed time, or whine the moment a family sits down to eat, in their frustration parents often lash out in anger at each other. It helps to remember that infancy is a temporary stage. Life will regain some sense of order before you know it. In the meantime, focus on being nice to each other by minding your manners. A simple "please" or "thank you" goes a long way toward making someone feel appreciated and can defuse an otherwise tense situation.

2. **Indulge in simple pleasures.** Does he like Merlot? Does she have a passion for chocolate-covered strawberries? Surprise each other with little gifts that each of you finds special.

3. **Take a family walk.** Either early in the morning before work or late in the evening as your twins are winding down, load them in the stroller and head out the door with your mate. Not only are you getting exercise, but it's a great opportunity to start a dialogue with your significant other.

4. **Meet for lunch.** Kids are optional.

5. **Seal it with a kiss.** Sweet love notes or "just thinking of you" memos strategically placed in a briefcase or posted on the bathroom mirror can turn an ordinary day into a special one.

come over for a few hours instead of hiring a stranger to care for your kids. This way you can slowly get used to the idea of someone else looking after your babies. You can return your friend's act of kindness by taking her to lunch or cooking her a meal. And once you've tasted a little adult freedom, I guarantee you'll want to begin the process of finding a more permanent solution to your babysitting needs.

The best way to find a qualified sitter is by word of mouth. Ask your neighbors with children for recommendations, ask coworkers, or post an ad on the job board at a local college (that's how we found our sitter who stayed with us for more than four years). Spread the word that you need a sitter through your local church, play group, or Mothers of Twins Club.

While most parents are happy just to find one qualified sitter, some prefer to hire two babysitters to care for their twins. While this is a prudent idea if your sitter is a high school student who might feel overwhelmed by the amount of attention two infants require, it can be a costly venture. And if your plans call for an evening outing after the babies are asleep, having two sitters is usually not necessary.

After the interviewing process is complete and the references have been checked, it's time to see how your new sitter relates to your twins. Invite her over and watch how she interacts with your kids. If the chemistry is good, schedule a trial run—leave the house for a short period of time. Do your twins seem happy upon your return? If so, chances are you have a winner. During the next few weeks, slowly build up your time away from home so that everyone has ample opportunity to adjust to the new situation.

Is Three a Crowd? Nurturing Sibling Relationships

We do try to have one-on-one time with our oldest son. Since he remembered how it was before having two baby brothers, we didn't want him to feel resentful of them. There were plenty of opportunities to do things with him alone from school projects to Cub Scouts.

We've all heard stories or know of a family in which the firstborn child has a difficult time adjusting to a new brother or sister. Now, just imagine that same child trying to adapt to the arrival of twins. Not only do twins garner special attention from parents, strangers, and relatives, but Mom and Dad are too tired to give the single child the attention that he or she needs and deserves. It isn't easy on parents either. They're

TOP FIVE THINGS EVERY BABYSITTER NEEDS TO KNOW ABOUT TAKING CARE OF TWINS

Found a sitter you like and trust? Great! But before you head out the door, make sure your new sitter is drilled in the basics of baby care, first aid, and the following twin-specific points.

1. **Twins' routine.** Does one child usually wake up from a nap earlier than the other and need to be removed from the nursery before waking his or her twin? Does the other need a pacifier to fall asleep? Write down your children's schedule, noting any caveats to their routine.

2. **Twins' names.** It's never easy for newcomers to learn which name goes with which baby (especially if your twins are identical). Help your sitter to easily identify each child by color-coding their clothes.

3. **Twins' temperaments.** Does one baby routinely cry when bedtime nears in preparation for sleep? Or does one twin have a more difficult time taking a bottle and must be coached into drinking? Explaining each baby's peculiar temperament will ease a new babysitter's anxiety that something is wrong with her technique.

4. **Twins' allergies.** They may look alike, but their bodies tell a different story. One baby may be allergic to regular formula and can have only soy formula. To ensure there are no mistakes at mealtime, label bottles carefully and pin a ribbon on the formula-sensitive child.

5. **Whose blankie is whose?** Even young babies have preferences. Label blankets and favorite toys until your sitter can easily identify whose is whose for herself.

drained from attending to their new babies' demands, and now their once-happy toddler has suddenly begun to act out at home and in school.

When the novelty of two new babies has worn off and the older sibling realizes that the new sisters will not be returning to the hospital, resentment can build. A young child forced out of the spotlight can resort to all sorts of attention-seeking behavior. It's not uncommon for the single child to throw tantrums or wet the bed. Often, the older sibling's behavior toward new siblings turns passive-aggressive as he or she deals with the inner turmoil—yelling in the house during the twins' naptime, hiding bottles of formula, or taking toys away when Mom or Dad aren't looking. Jealousy sometimes manifests itself through hitting and biting. Or when a single child sees the attention lavished on twins, that child may revert back to infancy by sucking a thumb or wanting to sleep in a crib. And the closer the singleton is in age to the new siblings, usually the more acute the problem.

It helps to realize that your older child is adjusting, too, and often lacks the tools to express frustrations. When children feel secure with their parents' love, they'll accept new siblings more readily. Nurturing your relationship with your older child (or children) well before and after the twins arrive builds trust and ultimately keeps the peace within a household.

Tips for Nurturing the Parent-Child Relationship

- **Spend special time together.** Make time every day (even if it's just 10 minutes) to spend a few moments alone with your single child doing something that he or she has chosen—reading together, snuggling, or playing a game.

- **Have realistic expectations.** Don't expect a hungry two-year-old to wait patiently for dinner while you nurse the twins. That two-year-old is, after all, a child too.

- **Avoid the "mommy's little helper" role.** Let an older sibling help when he or she wants to; avoid making too many demands. Remember, small children need constant supervision—never leave children alone to attend to babies.

- **Listen.** Acknowledge his or her anger, sympathize with frustration, and together come up with a solution.

- **Keep the routine consistent.** The days following the birth of twins are not the time to send your older child to preschool. (That child will feel as though you are trying to get rid of him or her.) Make changes in an older child's schedule months before the arrival of the twins.

- **Give special privileges.** There are perks to being the oldest, like staying up later and choosing what to have for dessert. Let your older child know that it sometimes pays to be the firstborn.

- **Protect privacy.** You may not mind if your twins pull clothes from your dresser drawers, but your five-year-old might. Let your older child tell you what's off-limits to new siblings.

- **Give lots of love.** Plenty of hugs and kisses go a long way.

The Postpartum Body

As the chaos of the first month begins to wane, moms of multiples slowly turn their attention more toward themselves—namely assessing their bodies. And many will ask, "After gaining 40-plus pounds, will I ever fit into my 'good jeans' again?"

Every mom I interviewed had a wry sense of humor surrounding her postpartum figure. It's really the healthiest way to approach the subject as the reality can be a bit sobering to most of us. A very few moms lost all their pregnancy weight within a few months of giving birth, but those were the women who breastfed or who were completely devoted to weight loss. Some moms who were overweight when they got pregnant actually lost weight with the birth of their children due to their highly controlled diets during pregnancy. (Hey, that's great news!) The majority of moms, however, said it took close to a year to lose the baby weight, and a few others said they're still trying to get those last stubborn pounds to take a hike.

But weight loss is only half the battle. Unfortunately, our bodies may never look the same again—many of the parts have shifted. Where there once was a proportioned set of hips, are now love handles. But the biggest problem by far is the extra loose skin encompassing our stomachs, lovingly referred to as "twin skin." Perhaps you've heard about it? Twin skin remains once your stomach has "deflated" from childbirth. And that's exactly how it looks—like a deflated balloon. Not a pretty image. But if you had to choose between big, healthy babies or a flat stomach, I'm sure like most of us, you'd choose the former.

"I am slowly losing the extra weight," one mom said. "But I have lots of loose skin and stretch marks. I prefer to think of those as battle scars, and I won the battle so I'm proud to have them."

Losing the extra weight will come with dedication and time, the twin skin, however, may require a different strategy. Although exercise (both cardio as well as resistance training) will help the overall appearance, it won't get rid of the excess skin. Surgery (a.k.a. a "tummy tuck") is one answer, albeit costly and not without risk. To reduce the stomach wrinkles, cure-alls abound from emu oil and Dead Sea salt scrubs to "dry skin brushing." Most are only temporary fixes. A few moms found a new laser technique called thermage to be promising, although its effectiveness is purely anecdotal at this point and the cost not much less than surgery.

Applause

Congratulate yourself—you successfully made it through the first six months of twinhood. Many of the problems that plagued you in the beginning (nighttime feedings and the 5 o'clock fussies) are just a fuzzy memory, and life seems to be settling down. But wait—the fun is just about to begin.

•6•

Months 7 Through 12

The first time they played together they were seven months old. They were supposed to be sleeping. I heard a ton of giggles so I quietly poked my head in their room. They were playing peek-a-boo. It was the cutest thing—I almost cried!

Developmental Milestones

Your twins are growing so fast! And during the next six months, they will undergo fascinating changes from crawling to walking, from babbling to speaking a word or two. It's also during this stage of development that your babies will slowly discover something even more important—each other.

Mobility is the name of the game for your active babies, so batten down the hatches. During the seventh month, your kids will find some way of getting around either by creeping or crawling, but some innovative explorers find that a succession of rolls also does the trick just fine. Babies are able to sit up by themselves by now, too. But stay close by —they won't be able to keep their balance for very long.

Socially, your twins still won't actively interact, say, by rolling a ball to each other; but you will notice that they often crawl into the same room and play side by side. This form of "parallel play" will continue past the first year or so. But don't think that they're not aware of each other—they are. Twins are often comforted by their counterparts in times of trauma, like when Mom or Dad leaves the room or at bedtime.

During the eighth month, curious little minds motivate babies to constantly be on the run. Never content to just hang out, your twins delight in crawling into every corner of the house and may even be able to pull themselves up (holding on to the furniture, of course) for a closer look at the contents on the tops of end tables. If you reprimand one for tugging at the lamp, the other curious sidekick is sure to crawl over to investigate what the fuss is all about. At mealtime, look for the pincer grasp as babies learn to coordinate their thumbs and forefingers to pick up small objects. That's not all they're figuring out either. Their little brains are busy learning how to solve simple problems, like how to crawl around large objects.

Cruising, or walking while holding on to furniture, is a big ninth month milestone and the next step toward mastering the art of walking solo. While it's amazing how far your little guys can travel by simply navigating along the furniture, their main mode of transportation is still crawling—now watch as they do it while holding objects in one hand. Those little hands have become useful tools, too. Babies this age delight in putting small objects inside larger ones, banging two articles together, or placing one toy on top of another.

As the ninth month progresses, babies will begin to understand what is being said to them, so talk it up! Simple questions like "Where's your shoe?" often bring interesting results and occasionally the shoe itself. As independent as they are now, some babies will exhibit distress if Mom or Dad leaves the room. And as one baby cries, the other will often join in, showing a sense of sympathy. Loving reassurance to all goes a long way to calming the situation.

You'll notice by the tenth month that each twin is at a different level of motor development. One may be cruising the furniture, moments away from taking the first unaided step, while the other is content with crawling and exploring the new frontier below. Not to worry, though— all babies (including twins) develop at different rates. By the eleventh month, he or she will have caught up with the co-twin in crime. And when that happens, look out—two tots on the move mean double trouble. When one gets into mischief, the other is sure to follow, both disobeying your disapproving comments. When you remove the item in question, their reactions will range from a guilty look to noisy rage and foot stomping. This, too, will pass as babies learn to control their emotions.

Your twins will be ready to "step into" their first birthday with distinct and different personalities. Independent and mobile, the babies have changed enormously since the day you first laid eyes on them 12 months ago. Your twins will continue to enjoy each other's company and parallel play throughout the day. At times you may wonder if they are aware of each other, but the next moment you notice them both laughing as they lie on top of each other. It's just the beginning of a long and special relationship.

The Exploring Twins

Once your babies are off and crawling, it can be a relief as well as a nightmare. No longer are you required to entertain your twins every waking moment; now they delight in making discoveries of their own, giving you a few moments to yourself. But many moms, including me, found this important milestone to be a huge adjustment. After all, when they were infants quietly dozing in their bouncer seats, it was easy to keep tabs on them. Once they became mobile, however, I no longer had full control over where they could go in the house or what they would do once they got there. Furthermore, there were many times when they would take off for separate rooms. While rearranging dangerous electrical cords and closing the bathroom door gave me some peace of mind, I would often scurry from room to room frantically shouting, "Where's your brother?" Many moms sympathize.

When I told another mom with twins of my dilemma, she turned me on to the "superyard," eight interlocking gates that form a large and safe play area. When the guys got out of control and I was tired of running after them, I housed them in their miniplayground with a host of toys. It worked great for a few months; that is, until they discovered that if they banded together, they could push the gates over and break out. So much for that idea. It's not uncommon, I later found out, for twins to work together as coconspirators to find an escape route out of cribs, playpens—you name it.

So how do you allow your twins to explore without driving yourself mad? First, remember that no matter what you do, your babies will continue to wander and investigate, and you need to become comfortable with this important stage of development. Next, decide what's acceptable behavior and what isn't and be consistent in teaching your children the rules. For instance, standing on furniture in our house was (and still is) a definite no-no (my fear was that they would fall and seriously hurt themselves), but rummaging through closets and dresser drawers was perfectly OK. Finally, find compromises that meet your kids' need to examine their new world and your need to keep them safe. Some families, for example, gate off certain rooms, either keeping their twins in or out.

Other parents insist that their house remain open territory and remove all tempting and potentially dangerous objects, thereby letting their kids roam at will. One thoughtful mom deals with wandering twins by encouraging them to follow her from room to room. When she needs to do dishes, she herds them into the kitchen and opens up a cabinet filled with plastic containers. "They stay occupied for a good 20 minutes, and I can actually get my dishes done and maybe get dinner started."

Babyproofing Your Home

Parents of twins have a tough job when it comes to keeping their children safe, since it's harder to keep track of two babies on the go. You may have one twin within your eyesight, but then suddenly you remember you haven't heard a peep from the other, who has quietly crawled off while you weren't looking. As you run through the house in search of the lost explorer, your other twin decides now is the best time to take a bite out of the electrical cord in the living room. Stressful, to say the least.

Once your twins begin to crawl, all cords, colorful pottery, and lamps are fair game in their curious eyes—so it's up to you to move such items and create a safe and child-friendly environment. Start by taking a tour of your house "baby-style"—on your hands and knees. From this unique perspective, potential hot spots become more obvious. Move all breakables to higher ground, and be on the alert for small objects that could cause choking, as well as electrical cords and lamps within reach. Obviously, you can't make your home an adult wasteland, void of knick-knacks and art. Some objects can't be moved (like books on low shelves), and babies must be taught through consistency that they are off-limits to prying little hands. But remember, for all the safeguarding you may do to your home, nothing takes the place of adult supervision. Never leave your children unattended for more than a moment. Babyproofing should never take the place of a responsible caregiver.

Childproofing Tips

- Cover sharp corners on coffee tables and fireplace hearths with padding. Move houseplants out of reach, discarding any that are poisonous. Secure heavy objects like televisions to prevent them from tipping over.

- Rearrange electrical cords so that babies can't tug at them. Replace electrical outlets with childproof outlet covers.

- Move babies' cribs away from draperies and miniblinds, where the potential for cord strangulation is great. Keep the night-light away from bedspreads, blankets, and draperies, where it could start a fire. Don't hang pictures or shelves above babies' cribs.

- Use safety latches to lock drawers and cabinets. Keep all sharp objects like tweezers, scissors, metal nail files, and pocket knives in locked drawers. Keep all over-the-counter and prescription drugs as well as household cleaners, matches, and other harmful substances in their original containers and in locked cabinets or on high shelves away from toddlers' reach.

- Install smoke alarms in each bedroom. Check them monthly and replace the batteries annually. If your home uses nonelectrical fuel (oil, gas, or coal), install a carbon monoxide detector in the hallway near the bedrooms.

- Keep the bathroom door closed when not in use. Use a nonskid rubber mat in the tub. To prevent accidental scalding, lower the water heater temperature to 120 degrees or less. And remember to never leave children unattended while in the bathtub, as they can drown in just a matter of seconds.

- Finally, post phone numbers for poison control and your pediatrician as well as the name and address of the nearest hospital on the refrigerator door. Educate yourself in first-aid basics and take a class in CPR (cardiopulmonary resuscitation; classes are available through your local Red Cross or the American Heart Association).

SAFETY ON THE GO

While you will need to take considerable time and effort to make sure your home is a safe haven for your babies, security while out and about is equally as important. These days, parents need to use caution as well as common sense when traveling to either the corner store or venturing into unfamiliar territory. One parent struggling alone with two young children in a poorly lit parking lot can be overwhelming, not to mention potentially dangerous, but following a few simple rules can help keep trouble at bay.

- Use the "last out/last in" rule when moving kids in and out of the car. When you arrive at the supermarket, for example, set up your stroller and then unstrap your kids from their car seats and put them in. Upon departure, unlock all necessary doors and the trunk, load your parcels into the car, and then strap the kids into their seats. Having your children close to you as long as possible protects them in case a malevolent stranger approaches the car. And never leave your children unattended in the car while you search for or dispose of a shopping cart.

- Keep the stroller or shopping cart next to you when getting kids in and out of the car. Never leave the stroller or shopping cart on the opposite side of the car where it is out of your sight. (When I was busy strapping one son into his seat, I often anchored one foot on the inside of the shopping cart so it wouldn't roll away.)

- Invest in portable seatbelts to properly secure kids in shopping carts (available from baby product catalogs). Since it's impossible to watch both babies while you shop, belting them in their respective carts prevents them from climbing out (and believe me, they'll try).

- Belt twins in separate carts or find a double cart when shopping. While it may be tempting to put two children inside the basket of one shopping cart, it's not a good idea. If one child stands in the cart and the side is lower than his or her chest, that child can easily tumble out (I also know this from experience).

Treating Twins as Individuals

I often refer to my older twins as my "guinea pigs," though not within their earshot or as an insult. In the past, I thought having twins was cute, and it was fun to trick people without realizing that my twins weren't getting a chance to be themselves. As a result they went through a stage where they disliked each other, based on people confusing them for each other. They hated being twins and resented being treated like one person. My younger twins, however, are happy to be separate or together—their individuality isn't an issue. I've taught them to correct people when they mistake them for the other. I try to spend one-on-one time with each twin as well as having time with them together.

When twins are born, parents initially bond with them as a unit, but as they spend time with their new children, moms and dads begin to bond with each child individually. Eventually, even parents of identical twins forget that their kids share the same biological makeup and see them as very different people as the twins display differences in personality and preferences. By focusing on these differences as well as nurturing them, parents in effect have begun to help mold their children's individuality.

Yet sometimes proud parents who want to emphasize their children's twinness refer to them collectively as "the twins," give them similar-sounding names, and continue to dress them in identical clothing throughout their toddler years. As the children get older and their differences become even more apparent, some parents discourage this for fear of breaking up the unit. By encouraging an interdependent relationship between twins, the pair has a more difficult time becoming independent adults. Yet our society highly regards independence, something that is difficult for twins to achieve when they are grouped together. In severe cases, interdependent twins either remain together as adults and never marry or are miserable living apart.

While the above example is extreme, a less obvious way parents compound the unit-thinking problem is by dealing with their children collectively. Admittedly, putting twins on the same schedule is a must for most families, but the twin as an individual gets overlooked in order to save time. For example, both children are fed at the same time, perhaps when only one is hungry. They're bathed together, and they go to bed at the same time.

Although establishing independence in your twins is important, you need not destroy their twinship by deliberately keeping them apart. The twin bond is an asset, a cherished friendship for life. If your children feel equally loved and cared for by you, then their individual personalities will naturally flourish.

They started their independence right from the start with my encouragement. I did my best to educate everyone on the importance of individuality. Now they pick out their own clothes and want different toys, and I encourage their different interests. Justin is all about sports while Josh likes to build things.

Top Five Ways to Establish Each Child's Individuality

Although twins share the same birthday and much of the same DNA, they are two unique people and deserve to be treated as such. Parents can help their children develop a healthy sense of self with these tips.

1. **Try not to refer to your children as "the twins."** Use each child's individual name, speak to each child directly and not as a group, and encourage family members and friends to do the same.

2. **Focus on their differences rather than their similarities.** If one child loves music while the other prefers sports, respect their differences and nurture their preferences. Never force both children into the same hobby or sport. However, if both truly want

to take piano lessons, don't persuade one to try the tuba for the sake of independence. Let them guide you.

3. **Foster privacy.** While it may not be possible to give twins their own rooms, allow each one to have private space. Whether it's an assigned drawer, a shelf in the closet, or a small corner in their shared bedroom, older twins need a place to call their own. Separate toys and separate books also give each child a sense of ownership, reinforcing individuality.

4. **Assign different chores.** Doing a separate household chore from a sibling builds a child's self-esteem by giving him or her a chance to contribute positively (and independently) to family life. When each child finishes a task, rather than jockeying for recognition, that twin can take pride in the accomplishment. He or she will gain confidence and learn to operate more independently.

5. **Allow each child to make a choice.** From the weekend video rental to the nightly bedtime story, rather than insisting that the vote be unanimous, allow each child to make a personal choice. Some families have implemented, "Star of the Day," where each child gets to make family decisions all day long.

• •

Even when parents are acutely aware of stressing individuality and actively guide their children along their chosen paths, sometimes family members aren't as quick to join in. Sometimes Grandma will continue to give matching clothes or the same birthday present to each child, for instance, or continue to call them "the twins" rather than addressing them individually. Part of the problem may be that she isn't aware that her actions could hinder their emerging autonomy. Enlighten her with a heart-to-heart conversation on your strategy for promoting your twins' individuality. Or perhaps she simply doesn't see her grandchildren often enough to help her distinguish between the pair. Make it easier for her by sending frequent separate photos of each baby dressed in different outfits complete with name written at the bottom so she can start to make individual connections. Better yet, ask her if she'd like to spend an afternoon with just one child (just be sure to give the co-twin equal time on another day).

SHOULD YOU SEPARATE TWINS FOR A DAY?

It's important to spend one-on-one time with our boys because I so very much want them to feel loved, and it's easier to accomplish when they don't have to share Mom's or Dad's attention. When one curls up in my lap for a movie or story, or walks with me alone through the grocery store, I feel that "affection connection," and I'm convinced he does, too.

I remember one of the first times I took one of my guys out alone without his co-twin. They were about 18 months old, and one volunteered to head to the store with me. As I was buckling Michael into his car seat, Joseph came running out to the car and tried to convince him to stay. He grabbed Michael's arm and tried to pull him out of the car. But Michael resisted and instead tried to persuade Joseph to come with us, so he grabbed his arm and pulled back. Within minutes they were yelling and crying, "Come!" and "No, stay!" I just stood back dumbfounded! I could see the pain in Michael's face (and not just from getting pulled from the car) as he wanted to go out alone with me, but he didn't want to leave his co-twin behind. Joseph, too, was upset at the thought of being without Michael. Even for a short time, it seemed like too much to bear.

I blame myself for that fiasco. When they were little, it was easier for us all to be together so I rarely took the time to separate them to run errands. Before long, I thought, they'll spend plenty of time apart. For now, if they want to be together, why not let them?

In those days, many parents of twins agreed, insisting that taking just one twin to the store and leaving a co-twin behind caused lots of fighting and whining with the "one left behind" spending the entire time crying.

These days, parents of twins are more in tune with the benefits of private time with each child. They realize getting out with just one twin at a time, even when the twins are just babies, allows parents to bond sooner and with more depth with each child. It's not only quality of time but quantity of time that cements their relationship. Each child gets to shed his or her twin title for the day as the spotlight shines solely on that child. When a child is separated from a twin, he or she feels more independent and appreciated for being, well, just himself. It wasn't until I had a singleton two years after my twins that I realized that fact. So now, like most double-duty parents, I regularly take each one of my sons out for an afternoon with just mom. (My husband, too, takes the boys out regularly.) But the benefits are reciprocal as my sons also get a chance to see me in a different light. Without the need to yell, "Knock it off! We're in public!" every other minute (remember, I have three boys), I can be the "nice mom," the one I always knew was inside me but just couldn't come out to play.

Double-duty parents are coming up with all sorts of ways to spend time alone with all their children, not just their twins. "Once a year we have what's called Mommy Day from School, where each child gets to play hooky and spend the day doing fun things like going to art museums," one very cool mom of five children explained. "We do this for each of our children. I fully attribute it to why my twins have such a healthy relationship now." Great idea! But this mom says it's only when her kids don't have scheduled tests or projects. Another mom takes only one child at a time to a mommy-and-me class.

As they get older and more used to the arrangement, most children realize it's not just the kid who goes out who has all the fun. The co-twin at home also gets a parent to himself or herself (or grandparent, aunt, or significant friend), free to play a game or simply snuggle and read.

But if you really want to tap into the latest trend, why not try vacationing with just one? Obviously you'll have to wait a few years to try it, but many parents say that the occasional, one-on-one minivacation is a way for parents and children to reconnect. "I took one son to the Montreal Jazz Festival for three days last summer," a mom of identical boys told me. "Then I took the other on an overnight trip to an island later in the summer." The benefit? "I got to know them as individuals and recognize their differences more than when they're together." Besides, she said, it's just plain easier when there's only one.

Many parenting experts think that mother-daughter or father-son vacations are a bit indulgent, stemming from parental guilt from working long hours and overscheduling children. Furthermore, since most kids are great scorekeepers, someone will always have an issue with what he or she didn't get to do (read: you spent more money on one child than the other).

Regardless, the payback for spending private time with each child is plentiful. If you want to try it, however, take the advice of those who have been there: If you start the process when babies are young and do it often, not only will your twins accept the practice as commonplace, eliminating many a teary scene, but you'll also reap the rewards, too.

To Dress Alike or Not to Dress Alike?

I love dressing them alike. Isn't that one of the perks of having identical twins? As for the whole "identity debate," I think that's silly. My boys are so different in personality that looking and dressing alike has no bearing on them as individuals.

In collecting surveys for this second edition, a few answers to twin-specific topics surprised me. This was one of them. In the past, whether to dress twins alike was often debated among parents of multiples, with each side having very strong views to back their decisions, but I thought with today's contemporary parents that this one was dead. I was wrong. Although parents of multiples don't dress their children alike as often as parents 25 years ago did, it's still very common, especially with parents of young twins.

Personally, I never dressed my boys alike even for special occasions or family photos. To me, dressing twins alike went hand in hand with the individuality issue—you can't stress the importance of autonomy in a child when there's an identically dressed child, his co-twin, mirroring back that he's not autonomous. It has to affect them on some level. A 2006 Canadian study concluded that, "In preparing their twins' bodies for public presentation, parents play a key role in communicating twin identity on their children's behalf." Moms and dads need to realize that although they have a strong sense of their children's individual identities and don't see them as one, the world just outside their door doesn't see two, identically dressed children as different. They don't try to make the connection. How can they when they're presented with two same-age children dressed alike?

Yet many parents disagreed, saying they loved dressing their children alike and saw no inherent problem with it. And for the first few months of your twins' lives, there isn't any harm as they won't be the wiser for it. But the Canadian study also pointed out that twins who dress alike often learn to behave as twins.

There are plenty of degrees to the issue, though. For instance, some parents only dress their twins alike for special holidays or photos; plenty of families dressed their twins in coordinating outfits—same style but different colors. Several confided that they were trying to wean themselves from the habit as their preschool children are beginning to protest. One mom based her decision on practicality. "I dress my twins alike in certain situations," she said. "Dressing alike is a great help when we go to places with crowds like Disneyland. It makes it easier to spot them and keep track of them."

TOP FIVE FAVORITE ACTIVITIES
FOR YOUNG TWINS

Before you know it, your twins will be fighting over who gets the family car on Saturday night, but for now, they want to play with only you. Keeping a baby happily occupied (let alone two) is no easy feat. Rather than another round of peek-a-boo, try these fun games.

1. **"Where's Dada?"** Help teach your children the names of people and things with this simple game of questions. Look directly at your children and ask, "Where's Dada?" Wait a moment, and then point to Dad and exclaim, "There he is!" In a short time, your children will begin to look or point at their father. When they do, congratulate them with kisses and cheers. Build the vocabulary list slowly and keep it short and simple: Mama, Dada, kitty cat, dog, and of course, parts of their bodies.

continued

2. **"I'm gonna get you!"** Once your babies learn to crawl, get down on your knees and crawl after them. They'll love it. When you catch one, hug, kiss, and roll around on the rug together; then release the twin. Watch as he or she quickly crawls off with every intention of being caught again. Not only will your babies' motor skills improve, but they'll become more aware of their own bodies as well.

3. **Floor play.** Get down on your babies' level—literally—for a little interactive play that your twins direct. Be an active participant by building block towers and turning the pages of a book, but be careful not to take control—let your kids guide the agenda. Floor time helps your children grow emotionally by offering a safe place where anything goes.

4. **Singing and hand clapping.** Babies love repetitive songs such as "Pat-a-Cake" or "The Wheels on the Bus." The rhythmical quality helps to build vocabulary and teaches simple motor skills like hand clapping. Researchers also say that singing to your baby helps build more pathways to the brain.

5. **Reading.** It's never too early to start reading to your children. And while reading to your babies helps them to do better once they hit school, trying to keep their attention for longer than five seconds is a real challenge. The secret to success is to find the right book, one with bright, colorful pictures and simple vocabulary (Dr. Seuss's Young Reader's Series is a great place to start). Keep the story short (no more than a few minutes), and give each of your babies a book to hold while you're reading (try using board books—they're harder for babies to destroy).

Life After Infancy

The whirlwind of the first six months is finished, and now the reality of parenting twins is slowly sinking in. For some families with older children, life as they knew it has returned, but for new parents, it's just the beginning of a changing evolution. New ground rules to the family's dynamics are being drawn up; there are changes to the family's social life (it isn't a coincidence that your new best friends just happen to have kids, too), changes to the marriage, and changes to the family's future plans.

KEEPING THE MARRIAGE ON TRACK

We also tried to keep our sense of humor throughout. Poop can be funny! Really! Just know that you can't control everything and just when you think you have "it" down, the "it" changes. Lean on each other as much as possible. Talk to each other about how you're feeling, what you're mad about, what's frustrating you, what you're scared about. Communication is key to your being good parents to your little ones and staying sane throughout the process.

Raising children can be all consuming for parents. By the end of the day, they're left with little time to think about connecting emotionally with their partners, let alone physically. And for parents of multiples, their states of exhaustion are, well, doubled.

So how does the arrival of twins affect a marriage? For some, the added stress can push an already shaky union over the edge. For others, feelings of resentment surface—Mom wakes several times during the night to feed and diaper the twins while Dad snores away in the next room, or Dad feels left out since all of Mom's energy and attention is focused on the new babies. It's no wonder that the divorce rate or level of dissatisfaction is higher in families with multiples.

Be it a nightly chat session or a weekly date complete with babysitter, husbands and wives must find one-on-one time just for each other. Parents need to work on their marriages to keep families whole. Children need and deserve a nurturing environment with both a mother and a father. By striving for a coherent and loving marriage, parents not only deepen their commitment to one another, but also set a positive example for their children to follow. When parents are happy with their union, the whole family is happier for it.

Tips to Keep the Marriage on Track

- **Concentrate on the positive.** Rather than focusing on the negatives in your marriage ("He drives me crazy when he leaves the dirty diapers in the nursery!"), reflect on your mate's positive qualities. Is he a good father? Is she a loving mother? Is he faithful? Is she truthful? Does he love to sing to the kids?

- **Call a meeting.** If your marriage is beginning to feel more like a corporation than a spiritual union, hold a board of directors meeting. Find a quiet time each week to talk and reconnect with your spouse. Discuss issues that are troubling you or pleasing you, or simply discuss the family's future. The point of a weekly or nightly gab session is not necessarily to complain, but just to check in with each other.

- **Find time to be alone.** Whether it is a date, a walk, or a shower together—make alone time a priority.

DAD'S CHANGING ROLE

My initial reaction was horror. Honestly, I leaned up against the wall in the ultrasound office and said the "F" word about four times. We were trying for one . . . how would we be able to do this? Then, reality set in. I looked deep into my wife's eyes and said, "We need a new car and a bigger house."

Upon learning that two bundles of joy are on the way, rather than thinking up names and what color to paint the nursery, fathers' thoughts often turn to money and how they need to stretch the family budget to accommodate a growing household.

When we first learned the news, I immediately started thinking about the responsibility. I was more concerned with the financial burden. When I heard the word twins, *I thought, wow, this is going to be expensive. This is going to hurt.*

Many fathers of singletons feel isolated after the birth of their child as mothers turn their attention to the new baby. While some dads of twins reported feeling neglected, the majority did not. Twins, they said, pushed them into an active caregiver role—a positive addition to their families' dynamics. In addition, the fathers said, they developed stronger bonds with their older children. When Mom is busy nursing the twins, Dad steps in and becomes primary caregiver to his older children.

Top Five Ways to Encourage Paternal Involvement

When a baby's on the way, Dad's involvement is important, but when twins show up, his participation is crucial to a smooth-flowing household. Here are some ways to get every father to join in.

1. **Be active during pregnancy.** Attend birthing classes together (even if your doctor suggests a cesarean delivery), ask your wife to schedule her prenatal visits so that you can go along, and plan and decorate the nursery together (or at least voice your opinion in her choices).

2. **Take time off from work after the birth.** The first few weeks following a twin birth are critical for bonding with your newborns. Don't miss out. Use up your vacation time, or take advantage of the Family and Medical Leave Act.

3. **Don't wait to be asked to do something.** While it's true that Mom ultimately runs the baby show, get to know the routine and pitch in with diaper changes and bottle feedings. Pick a chore like bathing, and make it your nightly ritual—just you and the babies.

4. **Help with bottle feeding.** If your wife is breastfeeding, talk about the option of giving a daily bottle of expressed milk to each of your babies.

5. **Give Mom a day off.** Push her out the door on a Friday night for a much-needed break and then take over. (Finally, you get to do things your way!)

Introducing Solid Foods

Around six months of age (longer for premature infants), your twins will be ready to graduate to solid food (many pediatricians caution against starting sooner for fear of obesity later in life). How will you know when they are ready? According to the American Academy of Pediatrics, you should look for these signs and then speak to your doctor:

- Babies have good control over their bodies. They can sit with support and can swallow easily without gagging.

- They weigh at least 13 pounds or have doubled their weight since birth.

- They still seem hungry after 8 to 10 breastfeeding sessions daily, or 32 ounces of formula.

- They watch with great fascination as you eat.

FEEDING YOUR TWINS

Feeding twins can be just as easy as feeding one, or it can end up a messy disaster. Although I used my sons' copycat competitiveness to my advantage at mealtime, it did sometimes backfire. When Joseph turned his nose up at vegetables, I ignored him and loudly praised Michael for eating his carrots. Before long, my fussy eater decided that he was starving and concluded he liked his carrots after all. Unfortunately, the reverse was also true. If Michael threw his cup, Joseph would immediately follow suit. And if I dared reproach one for deliberately dropping fruit on the floor, I might as well go get the broom—his brother was sure to do the same.

During your first attempts at feeding your babies, try sitting them in their car seats instead of propping them in high chairs. As they get older and can easily sit without support, move them to high chairs or clip-on chairs.

And what about high chairs? Investing in two is expensive and takes up a lot of floor space. Some families combat this problem by buying one high chair and having babies take turns eating. This works fine during the first few months (except when both babies are irritable from hunger and both want to be fed *now*), but when babies are old enough to sit at the table with the family, someone clearly gets left out (or ends up sitting on someone's lap). Buying two clip-on chairs (portable chairs that secure directly onto the table) is a clever alternative. Not only are they cheaper than high chairs, they don't take up valuable dining room floor space and are compact enough to take on the road.

The easiest and fastest way to feed babies is at the same time. Simply share one bowl and one spoon. Sit between them and alternately give each child a bite. While this makes a parent's job infinitely quicker than using two spoons and two bowls, babies have a greater chance of catching a cold or flu from each other since symptoms rarely show up in the first 24 hours. But however you choose to proceed, make cleanup easier by using newspaper instead of plastic under their chairs. One mom opted for using a cloth sheet under her twins' chairs. "I could just shake it outside and throw it into the wash," she explained. "I preferred the sheet to plastic because with plastic I would still have to wipe up spills. Fabric absorbed a lot of liquid."

Eating on Their Own

Never be in a rush to introduce solid foods to your babies. Believe me, the novelty of watching their reactions to their first taste of food quickly wears off as the drudgery of wiping dried spaghetti off the walls sets in. Fortunately, most twins tire of waiting their turn to be fed and learn to

feed themselves sooner than singletons. Not with forks or spoons, mind you, but they can do very nicely with finger foods—bite-sized pieces of cheese or well-cooked nuggets of vegetables or meat. When they do show interest in using a spoon, however, encourage and praise their efforts even though most of the food will wind up on the floor instead of in their mouths. And as you scrub the kitchen floor for the third time that day, just remember, you're one step closer (albeit a messy one) to your twins' eating independently.

As they get older, you might want to move your two epicureans farther apart at the table. Once twins discover an overhand throw, they'll spend most of mealtime catapulting peas at each other. Remember, too, that although they enjoy sharing mealtime together, babies will often have different taste preferences. Don't get troubled when one child prefers carrots while the other insists on eating only corn. Just continue to offer a wide variety of fruits and vegetables, and eventually their tastes will mature and expand. And someday, God willing, they'll even ask for a second helping of lima beans.

What a Year It's Been!

So much has happened during the past year. Not only have your twins grown from sleepy little cherubs to active, inquisitive toddlers, but you have undoubtedly done some changing, too. After all, who can calm two babies at once quicker than you? And did you ever think you could get them both fed and dressed and out the door in time for their afternoon play date? Those are not easy feats. Now, if you can only make it through toddlerhood and the dreaded terrible twos!

o 7 o

The Toddler Years

*I was getting the two of them dressed when the doorbell
unexpectedly rang. When I ran downstairs to answer it, they
helped each other get undressed again, and then traipsed
downstairs stark naked to find me talking to a deacon from
our church who had come to remind me to sign them up for
Sunday school.*

And they're off! The toddler years are a great time for families with twins—that is, if Mom and Dad can keep up. While it's fascinating to watch your dynamic duo develop and change, the toddler years can be exhausting, too. Preschool twins are constantly on the go, pairing up together to get into all kinds of mischief.

Developmental Milestones

Following your babies' first birthday, you'll struggle to keep up with their boundless energy. In constant motion, your pair may have mastered the art of climbing, so don't be surprised if they make it out of their cribs and into your room one night. This is also the age when their "twinness" becomes more apparent—an enchanting time indeed. Inseparable buddies, your kids will spend their morning chasing each other around the yard or rolling together on the living room floor. Twins are amazingly sensitive to each other's needs as well. If you offer one twin a treat, he'll often give it to his sibling first before taking one for himself. They may not nap or even go to bed at night unless their counterpart is close at hand.

It's the age of imitation, too. If you reprimand one for pulling the dog's tail, beware—the other is sure to do the same. It doesn't matter that he, too, gets scolded for the deed; his copycat behavior gets him exactly what he wants—attention from you. And that's just the beginning of your toddler-times-two headaches. Twins notoriously encourage each other to push the envelope just a little further. While in the park, a one-year-old singleton will venture only a few feet away from Mom or Dad, but twins acting together tend to be braver, sometimes wandering so far away that you'll wonder if they're ever coming back.

By 18 months, your twins can usually point to a variety of body parts when asked and can understand simple commands. Babbling begins to take the form of true words, and boy, do toddlers love using the few they know—especially with each other. You'll often overhear them in a serious but primitive conversation with one another. Are they really communicating? While some twins develop a private language that only they can understand, the chances are rare. Most likely your pair is merely practicing for the time when they really can talk to each other.

Well into toddlerhood by two years old, many twins develop very definite roles within their relationship. You'll clearly see that one is the leader, always forging ahead into uncharted territory with the follower just steps behind. There's no need to worry that these roles are permanent, though. As your twins begin developing a sense of self over the next few years, their intratwin roles are bound to flip-flop. You'll also witness the two seesaw in their developing talents. One child may be a master articulator, bombarding you with his or her particular insights on the world, while your other twin may be more reserved, content to spend the morning quietly building block towers. Once again, there's no need for concern. Every individual (even twins) tends to fluctuate in his or her abilities throughout life.

For the typical three-year-old, play and imagination come in many different forms, from imaginary friends to naughty phantoms who kick over the flowerpots. But when preschool twins team up, they often invent award-winning tall tales. While it may seem like lying to some, exaggeration is actually a normal stage of development. When playing together, young twins also like to change their identities. No longer content with the names Jill and John, you suddenly find that you are living with Miley Cyrus and Kobe Bryant. This harmless form of imaginary play can test the patience of parents when the two refuse to come to dinner until addressed by their new names.

By age four, your twins will begin to show more self-control. It's a welcome relief for parents as their twins learn to cooperate better and share toys with each other, but this is also the time when kids love to test boundaries, much to their parents' chagrin. "No" becomes a preferred word, and when you double that, you may feel like it's the terrible twos all over again. By now, many twins have become more social, requesting to play with others compared to playing with just each other. "We have no one to play with" becomes a favorite rainy-day expression. Yet many twins are still content to play within their own tight-knit circle of two. While it may be easier for parents to just let the two of them play, it's important to expand their circle of friends by introducing twins to other children their own age. Not only will this help them prepare for school, but twins who play with other children develop better speech.

As Toddlers Grow—Singing the Naptime Blues

They quickly figured out they could jump out of bed and run around and turn the lights on, causing havoc. We had to secure their bedroom several times, putting a latch on the closet (not before one had to go to the emergency room to rule out a broken pinky after her sister closed it in the door), and attach the furniture to the walls with straps.

Just when you thought all was going well—your twins are sleeping through the night so you are, too, and they're eating table food so you are no longer lugging baby food around everywhere with you—but then *bam!* Although they're exhausted from a morning of exploring, many twins just won't cooperate during naptime. The biggest problem, parents say, is that most doppelgängers have figured out that they can whoop it up together! Some of their stories sound more like a prison break than naptime. "They would get out of bed and dump their dresser drawers, rip window shades off the rollers, empty the laundry hamper, and tip over the rocking chair," one tired mom complained. Desperate, these parents finally emptied the contents of the room, leaving just the crib from which their boy-girl twins then stripped off the sheets and mattress pads.

So how do you get these overly tired toddlers to bed? Here are some tried-and-true tips from parents in the trenches:

- **Keep the crib.** Don't be hasty in moving your kids from cribs to toddler beds. Keep their cribs for as long as possible. If they're starting to climb out, move the crib away from furniture and lower the mattress as far down as it can go, making it more difficult to get out (one mom moved it to the floor). Or try a crib tent.

- **Remove distractions.** From the music box to teddy bears, remove whatever your kids find entertaining at naptime. If your rebels still won't cooperate, do as many parents have done and remove all the furniture! Your kids need to know you mean business and naptime is not party time.

- **Separate them.** Two tots in two separate locations will do the trick. Many parents use their pack-n-plays for this purpose. Although one mom said she wishes she could get hers out of her home office during naptime, it's there to stay until her girls give up their naps completely. Another mom of two sets of twins splits her Fab-Four all around the house. "Currently our four-year-old twins are split between their room and the guest room. Our one-year-old twins are divided between their room and a pack-n-play in the master bedroom closet," she explained. "The closet sleeper actually naps best. It's so quiet and dark in there!"

- **Use duct tape.** Yes, you read it right. As part of their stall tactic, many toddlers remove their diapers in protest. Wily parents fight back by duct-taping the diaper on with the end tab in back so junior can't rip it off.

From Two Naps to One

The time will ultimately come when your young toddlers will give up a nap, and it is often the case that one child will want to do it sooner than the other. For those of you who have your twins on the same schedule, shifting to one nap a day can be more of an adjustment for you than for your kids. So what should parents do?

Toddlers give up a nap at anywhere from 12 to 18 months. The majority give up their morning naps, but some, like mine, slept soundly during the midmorning but refused to go down in the afternoon. You'll know a scheduling adjustment is needed when you peek into the nursery every afternoon to find one child up and playing in the crib, while the other is snoozing soundly. If you want them both to continue on the same schedule, do you make both give up the nap? Or do you force one to lie down even though he or she is not tired? The answer all depends on you.

If one twin still needs a short second nap in the afternoon and the other twin is content to play quietly in the crib for the duration, count yourself lucky. There's nothing wrong with a little quiet time for everyone (this is how I handled it for a full year). If this is not the case, give the awake child some one-on-one time—often a rarity between twins and their parents. Let the child who needs a nap sleep while you enjoy a special hour alone with the other. Yet a third option is to switch both children to one nap and deal with the moody consequences. The toddler who didn't get a second nap usually becomes fussy at dinner or during the evening bath. Are you prepared for that? Still another alternative is to move the midmorning nap later and later each week until it becomes an afternoon nap.

Exploring the Twin Bond

Do twins really share some mystic bond? Many of us imagine they do. Are the minds of twins somehow wired together in utero or is this "psychic connection" manufactured by those of us who insist that twins be clones, exact body and soul images of each other? Identical twins share 100 percent of the same DNA, so many similarities in behavior and idiosyncrasies are inborn. But identicals are only one-third of the twin population. What about fraternal twins who only share 50 percent of their genes at most? Two siblings merely sharing the same birthday have their twinship thrust upon them. Comparisons are made between the two, however unfairly, simply because they share the title of "twin." Through common experiences, though, even they develop a bond that two siblings of different ages rarely achieve. Perhaps their relationship isn't as tightly woven as their identical counterparts, but the fraternal friendship can be strong nonetheless.

Many believe that the sibling connection begins in utero. Always maneuvering for space, twins have a prenatal experience that is vastly different than that of a singleton. About Week 10, twins in the womb become interactive partners with contact becoming inevitable and almost constant at about Week 15. Through ultrasound, doctors have observed twin fetuses fighting—one twin literally punching or pushing the other—as well as hugging. Competing as well as cooperating—two heads of the twin coin. During this prenatal period, the two are linked physiologically as well. Through nonstress tests (NSTs), researchers have shown that twins' fetal heart rates (FHR) are linked as the in utero pair show simultaneous periods of reactivity and nonreactivity.

But do monozygotic (identical) twins differ in their in utero behavior compared to dizygotic (fraternal) twins? Ultrasound reveals that although monozygotic twin fetuses are independent—each showing a different level of activity throughout pregnancy—they actually interact more than dizygotic fetuses during early gestation (at approximately Week 20 they reach the same level). Why is this? Could it be since some identical fetuses share the same amniotic sac and others have a very thin septum dividing the two that they have greater access to each other? Or is it something more?

Sacred and mysterious, the twin bond may never be fully deciphered, but as parents of twins we will continue to observe our children and try to explain the unexplainable.

The Beginning Bond

I noticed their bond when they moved them to the second level NICU and they were able to cobunk. Their vital levels seemed to regulate faster, and their breathing improved.

Many newborn twins take comfort in the close proximity of their co-twins. For instance, several parents told me that their neonatal intensive care unit (NICU) babies responded well—their vital signs stabilizing—when the two were placed side by side. "Brayden had problems with his body temperature staying up for any length of time," explained one mom. "The minute we put Mara, his co-twin, in the same bassinet at the hospital, Brayden's temperature went back to normal."

Researchers have observed that while many monozygotic newborns are soothed when placed together, many dizygotic infants become downright irritated when having to share a small space such as a bassinet, much to the disappointment of their parents. "Everyone told us to keep the girls in the same crib. They told us the girls would love it. Well, they didn't," one mom told me. "After two months of constant waking up, we put them in separate cribs. It was the first time they slept through the night."

Although twins, fraternal or identical, rarely actively interact during the first year, we wait anxiously for them to connect as twins and notice each other for the first time. Parents describe how during the first year, physical interaction between twins is usually limited to brief moments of discovery and manifested in the form of hand-holding or shared thumb-sucking. (It's important to note that singletons don't actively play with other children during their first year either.) "When we put them in the crib together at home, it was like they missed each other," explained a mother of identical twin boys. "Within a moment, someone's hand or foot was out of the swaddle and touching the other. It was fun to watch to see who was going to get free first and move over."

At around Month 4, twins may giggle in unison while lying in a crib together, or once they learn to crawl, they may momentarily chase each other around the nursery, but the majority of interaction or twin bonding parents report is subtle.

Following the first 18 months, twin toddlers move slowly from parallel play to more actively interacting with each other, though by the time the duo reaches three years old, they sometimes develop a love-hate relationship. Parents of twins often become disappointed when their twins fight even though they wouldn't think twice if two different-aged siblings engaged in a confrontation. All children within a family fight; it's just that twins and their relationship with each other are more closely scrutinized by those around them. As twins grow and mature, parents shouldn't try to prevent this sibling rivalry. Some of it is normal, and if parents try to eliminate it, it's bound to just fester underneath the surface instead.

Furthermore, not every set of twins will become best friends or inseparable buddies, at least not in the beginning. Many parents told me of their children's varying dispositions and personalities and how it played out in the context of the intratwin relationship. "Our twins have never really had that 'special connection' that other twins seem to have," said one parent of her fraternal boys. "One twin played better with our older son than he did with his twin. At age four, each got to spend a week at my mother-in-law's. Being apart didn't seem to upset them."

Even with the inevitable in-house fighting that parents report, however, there are many moments of concern, compassion, and cooperation between twin toddlers as they freely give each other juice cups or cookies, or comfort the other in times of pain. In my house, it was not unusual for one son to pick up two toys and then spend several minutes searching for his brother just to hand him one. No two same-aged toddlers that I've ever seen have such moments of cooperation. Another mom told me that when one of her twins cried, the other would take the pacifier out of his own mouth and put it in his co-twin's mouth to calm her.

With each passing month, you'll watch your growing twins gravitate closer to each other—the cornerstone of a unique and special relationship. During the early years, preschool twins—whether fighting or hugging—spend more time with each other than anyone else (including Mom or Dad). And while it's a relief for tired parents when twins play with each other on a daily basis, it's this type of forced bond, experts say, that's troubling—for many twins miss out on the relationship with their parents that they would have naturally cultivated if they had been born a single child. Therefore, it's important not only to nurture the twin bond, but also to nurture the parent-child relationship by finding time alone with each child every day.

NATURE VERSUS NURTURE THEORY

We all know that monozygotic (and some dizygotic) twins look remarkably alike, but why is it that so many have similar dispositions, personalities, and mannerisms? That's what the nature-nurture theory asks. What makes us who we are? Are we a product of our genetic makeup (nature) or of our environments (nurture)? When identical twins, who are genetic clones, are separated at birth, will they grow up to be completely different individuals, each becoming a product of their environments? Or will genes take over instead, influencing the same behavior in each?

Since 1979 psychologist Thomas Bouchard of the University of Minnesota and his colleagues have been studying both identical and fraternal twins who were separated at birth or in infancy and raised by different families as part of the now famous Minnesota Study of Twins Reared Apart project. More than 130 sets of twins who were adopted into different families at birth and then reunited as adults as well as those twins who grew up along side one another have been probed, prodded, and put through a battery of psychological and personality tests to see if genetics or environment answers the question of who we are.

Through their research they discovered that identical twins who were raised separately were very similar in intelligence, behavior, and personality. In fact, they had just as strong a chance of being as similar as identical twins who lived in the same home. So how could it be that so many twins reared apart could be so similar even though they never had any life experience together? Researchers concluded that it was their shared genetic makeup that was responsible for their likenesses. Furthermore, since genes account for similarities, it's the environment that actually carved out monozygotic twins' differences. But what's even more interesting is that it's just the opposite for fraternal twins. It's their collective environment that makes some of them seem more similar than genetics would suggest.

Speech Development

There's nothing sweeter than hearing "Mama" and "Dada" spoken for the first time. But did you know that toddlers around the world babble in the same way? It's not until parents hear words in their particular languages and then encourage their children to repeat those certain sounds that babies make the connection that the words they are babbling actually have meaning.

HOW LANGUAGE BEGINS

Your twin may not say much, but an infant from the moment of birth studies the way his or her parents communicate. As Mom and Dad raise and lower the pitch of their voices, or speak louder or softer to express varying emotions, baby is listening intently, storing the information until he or she can use it successfully.

At approximately four months of age, a baby begins "cooing," dropping and raising the voice and vocalizing open vowel sounds like "ooohhh" and "aahhh." The consonants B, D, M, and P follow next as baby babbles "Mama" and "Dada" for the first time. Then by six months, baby makes the connection that "Da-da" corresponds to that guy with the moustache who's been giving the bath every night. Baby now knows that words have meaning and actually responds to his or her own name when called.

THE FIRST WORDS

Soon after the first birthday, a baby speaks his or her first words. During this holophrastic period, when one word represents entire sentences, baby's pronunciation may not be exact. "Kiki" for *kitty cat* and "nana" for *banana* isn't perfect English, but baby will be consistent when referring to a particular object. The telegraphic phase, or two-word sentences, begins during baby's second year. Speech at this time is similar to a telegram (hence the name "telegraphic")—baby uses only the important words in a sentence, leaving unimportant ones out. "Bye-bye Dada" and "Baby done" may be simple, but these endearing words speak volumes.

As a child participates in family life, he or she begins to understand that all social situations have "scripts" and soon pairs the scripts with the language baby hears, thus learning the meanings of expressions. By conversing with adults and participating in the community around them, most preschool children have learned how to use grammar and language to accomplish communicative tasks.

Tips to Aid Language Development

- Talk it up. Research has shown that quantity counts. The more words a child hears from birth to age three, the higher the IQ and the better the child will do academically in school. (Sorry, but putting your twins in front of TV and DVDs doesn't count.) Shoot for 30,000 spoken words a day—that's about the equivalent of reading *Goodnight Moon* 198 times!

- Another study found that encouraging children to engage in imaginary play helps with language acquisition and builds stronger vocabulary.

- Show your children family photos and tell them the names of things and people in the background. When taking your twins for a walk, point at objects and identify them. ("Look! It's a yellow flower.")

- Use opportunities during bath time, mealtime, and diaper changes to talk to your babies. Give them a running commentary of what you're doing: "Now, Mommy's going to open the shampoo bottle and put a little in her hand. Then I'm going to rub it in your hair!" Even though they can't answer, ask them questions. ("Do you like the smell of the shampoo?") It not only builds vocabulary, but it teaches them about interactive conversation.

- Sing simple, rhythmic songs. Sit and read with your children every day.

- Introduce your twins to sign language. Some speech experts feel that infants have an instinctual need to communicate, and that teaching babies to sign enhances their conversation skills, lessening children's communication frustration. There are plenty of books on the subject—check your library or do an Internet search.

Speech Difficulties in Twins

Many past studies have confirmed that language development in twins lags behind that of singleton children. Although their receptive skills are on par with single-born kids (i.e., they understand what is being said to them), some twins' expressive language is mildly to severely delayed. By age three, for instance, twins on average are behind by 3.1 months. It's important to note that speech delay is not due to lack of cognitive development, but rather from the unique family situation in which twins find themselves. (It is important to note that singletons, too, are affected by some of these factors and can also develop speech problems. Twins, however, are just more prone to them.)

Some twins have a more difficult time developing their speech than the average child, due in large part to a lack of verbal involvement by their exhausted parents. Studies have shown that parents of twins not only speak less to their children than parents of singletons but their conversations are shorter, more directive, and less inquisitive. In other words, parents of twins stick to the basics: "Come here" or "Let's eat lunch," rather than asking in-depth questions and taking the time to wait for the answers.

Twins also spend a large portion of the day with each other, modeling each other's poor articulation (another reason to expose twins to other peers). In some situations, one twin will become the representative for the pair, while the other stands quietly by, content to let the co-twin answer for him or her. In this situation, rather than carrying on a one-on-one dialogue with each child, these parents are having a three-way conversation with their twins, further complicating their children's quest for language.

Speech delay usually diminishes from age 5 to 10, but the problem may have already negatively impacted other areas of a twin's life—namely in poor reading skills. Research shows that children with normal cognitive abilities but who are delayed in language acquisition are more likely to struggle to learn to read. The cause is still unclear.

IS THERE A SECRET TWIN LANGUAGE?

Some twins develop their own private language called "autonomous speech" or "twin language," where signs, words, and expressions are known only to the pair and can't be understood by other family members. Only a small percentage of multiples truly develop twin language (most of what parents report hearing is actually a form of immature speech). It usually shows up around age three and lasts for an average of 10 months. Furthermore, studies have shown that those twins who engage in frequent nonverbal play (playing that doesn't involve language such as painting or drawing), don't have an older sibling with whom to communicate, or don't attend preschool are at a much greater risk of developing it. While it's not necessarily harmful for twins to engage in autonomous language, it shouldn't be encouraged as it can lead to language delay.

ARE YOUR TWINS ON TARGET?

Check out these verbal milestones to make sure your twins' speech is on target. If they haven't hit their second-year milestones, have them evaluated by a speech pathologist. Remember most babies understand many more words than they can speak.

> **6–12 months:** Can babble "Ma-ma," "Da-da," and even "bye-bye." Tries to communicate through gestures, and enjoys repeating sounds.
>
> **1 year–17 months:** Can say a few words, but pronunciation may be unclear. Able to tie the words to objects or people. Tries to imitate simple words.
>
> **18 months–2 years:** Can say 8 to 10 words by 18 months, mostly nouns, although pronunciation may still be sketchy. Can say simple sentences like "All gone," and imitate animal noises like "woof." Starts to say pronouns like "mine."
>
> **2–3 years:** Can say about 50 words starting at age two but quickly amasses up to 200 by third birthday. Can say more pronouns such as "his" and "hers." Can string three-word sentences together. Uses inflection when asking a question.

Tips to Avoid Twin-Speech Problems

We try to foster their individual language skills by asking them about their day and reading to them separately, and giving each child a chance to speak even if they are telling the same story so that one doesn't speak for the other. We also approach the most mundane things in life as a learning opportunity—counting each stair as we carry them up and down, singing the spelling of each of their names or of our address.

- Insist that each child speak for himself or herself, applauding all efforts at communicating; never allow one child to become the spokesperson of the group.

- Never interrupt a child who is speaking to correct pronunciation. Instead, when the twin is finished, model the words correctly. "You said you like the dog? I do, too." Don't abbreviate words. *Bottle* is "bottle," not "ba-ba."

- Continue to read aloud to your children, and provide lots of imaginary play using dolls and hand puppets.

- Frequently repeat important words and phrases.

- Don't react instinctively to all of your children's needs; allow them to vocalize their desires. And if one child asks for something, allow the other child a turn to ask as well.

- Allow your twins to play with other children, and expose them to other adults. That's where preschool and/or play groups come in very handy.

The Terrible Twos—Are They So Terrible?

By the time my guys were 15 months old, they began to wear me down daily. With two strong wills and separate, distinct opinions, Michael and Joseph decided to test the limits a bit early. From the surveys I received from other parents, I realized that I was not alone.

Banding Together for Mischief

One winter day I made the mistake of staying on the phone for more than 30 seconds. Patrick and Rebecca used my lapse to run out of the house—barefoot in the snow—and hop into the car. They started opening and closing the garage door with the remote. When I ran out to get them (also barefoot), they locked the car doors and put the garage door down so not only couldn't I get to them, but I couldn't get back into the house to get my car keys!

Twins can think up all kinds of mischief, and if it's true that there's strength in numbers, parents had better be on their toes. While writing this second edition, I heard all kinds of twin legends, many downright shocking! Some mischief makers loved to paint each other and their bedrooms with Vaseline or baby oil. One mom recounts the day that her boy-girl twins dumped baby powder over each other's heads. "What a white wonderland," she laughed before she took a picture.

Another pair of preschool pranksters took a bunk-bed ladder from one bedroom into theirs, climbed up to the top of their dresser, got a jar of diaper cream, and then proceeded to paint their room. (What planning and execution!) "The stains on my carpet have faded but still haven't come out," the mom said. "Their clothes were ruined, but thank goodness it came off the walls and furniture."

There were tales of great teamwork as both twins worked together to get the candy from the top cabinet shelf or open refrigerator doors to help themselves to whatever caught their fancy. One twin even acted as a lookout as the other dismantled the baby gate to open up a forbidden zone. But still, my favorite story is about a pair of opposite-sex twins who filled up buckets of water and then dumped them into the master bedroom walk-in closet. "They wanted to create a pool," their mom explained. Sadly, her wooden floor was ruined as well as a few pairs of shoes. "The worst part was explaining it to the repairman. I'm sure he felt I wasn't watching my children carefully, but he'd never experienced twins!"

A Question of Discipline

They say twin toddlers hear the word *no* more often than the average child. Think about it—a twin hears no when it's spoken directly to him or her, he or she also hears it when it's meant for the counterpart, and he or she hears it when it's focused on the pair. With this in mind, it's no wonder that twins have a more difficult time internalizing house rules—they develop an immunity to the word *no* early on.

In the eyes of twins, no can lose its meaning very quickly. Therefore, the word should be used judiciously, and parents should choose alternate phrases instead. "Don't do that" and "Stay away from there" are effective alternatives. A reprimand, such as "Don't hit the kitty," should be followed with a better option of what to do: "Be nice to the kitty. Give her a kiss." Then loudly praise the good deed.

Although disciplining twins should follow the same rules as disciplining a singleton (setting limits, consistency, and so on), it is more difficult to discipline two toddlers at once. When two little tykes are fleeing the scene of a crime in opposite directions, it's often difficult to pinpoint the culprit. If neither child confesses to the misconduct, do you punish both? What if you suspect one child is taking the blame for the other, but you can't be sure? Then what do you do? And when you do finally nab one in the act, the close bond that twins often share sometimes makes it difficult to punish the offender—the "innocent party" may comfort the "guilty party," making the parent out to be the bad guy. Or, if both are punished, they may blame each other, exacerbating an already stressful situation.

Short of sending them off to military school until their 18th birthday, here are some ways to deal effectively with twin discipline.

- Reprimand the wrongdoer (or doers) in private to avoid embarrassing one twin in front of the other.

- Time-outs should be in separate rooms to prevent one twin from entertaining the other.

  I put Luke in a time-out once for hitting Jack. Luke was sitting there, and Jack came up with a stuffed bear and handed it to him. I'm thinking, He just hit you and you're bringing him a toy!

- Give more attention to good behavior with positive reinforcement in the form of praise and lots of hugs.

- Suggest a positive alternate behavior to an inappropriate one.

- Never punish both unless you've witnessed both misbehaving. Questioning both children separately and privately often gets to the heart of the matter, illuminating the true wrongdoer.

- Separate them. Even if for only a minute, separating sparring twins gives everyone a chance to cool off.

- Set a good example. Learning to share is a difficult concept for children under age two. Help them learn to take turns by eagerly sharing your "toys" with them. Let them see you share with other adults in your household. ("Look! Mommy and Daddy are sharing the newspaper.")

- React to each child's behavior individually, not as a group.

- If you accidentally accuse the wrong child, apologize.

FIGHTING BETWEEN TWINS

In the early years, fighting between twins is a daily occurrence and a strain on parents, who are forced to mediate. While twins rarely want to intentionally inflict physical harm on each other, they do often resort to biting, kicking, and pushing out of frustration. They don't realize that their fighting could have adverse effects. It's important that twins learn how to settle their own squabbles, but it will take patience and consistent teaching of the rules from parents.

Rather than taking an authoritative role when mediating twin fighting, experts suggest parents not get involved in their children's squabbles (at least not right away). They should detach themselves from the situation and instead become clarifiers and amplifiers. Instead of moralizing the behavior ("It's not nice to hit your brother!") or threatening the action with punishment ("If you hit him one more time . . . "), parents should clarify and confront by modeling what each child has said.

Michael: "Mom! Joe just hit me!"
Mom: "Joe, Mike said that you hit him."
Joe: "I hit him because he took my toy away."
Mom: "Mike, Joe said that you took his toy away."

Eventually, the children will talk directly to each other, bypassing the parent and often settling their own disagreements.

Tips to Ease Fighting Between Twins

- Do not intervene right away. Constant rescuing won't teach kids how to deal with conflicts on their own. Instead, observe from a distance to determine if the injured party is actually the instigator. Can the real victim deal effectively with the aggressive sibling by resisting or simply moving on to something else? If so, keep your distance.

- Never allow hitting, biting, or kicking. Immediately remove the offending party from the room and then comfort the injured party. Separation is the best way to teach a child that certain behavior is not acceptable.

- If twins fight over a toy, give the toy a time-out and suggest alternative toys.

- Twins often successfully share smaller toys such as puzzles, but large toys such as tricycles and dolls pose a problem. It isn't fair to expect a toddler to wait his or her turn for an extended period of time to ride a bike or play with a truck. At about 18 months, allowing twins to have their own toys cuts down on competition and fights. All children like to have something that they can claim as their own property.

TOILET TRAINING

My daughter wanted to try toilet training at around two years old and she did great. My son had zero interest. I tried once or twice a year to train him, but it wasn't until he really felt ready that we gave it a serious effort. So my son and daughter trained two years apart from each other!

Toilet training, one of the most sensitive areas of your twins' development, should be a pleasurable experience for everyone. As your twins gain control over their own bodies, using the toilet is their first official indication that they are entering the "big kid" world. Teaching twins the magic of the potty is the same as teaching a singleton. And as any parent with older children will tell you, if you begin too early, the whole process will backfire, causing anxiety for your twins and frustration for you.

When to Begin Toilet Training

Children have physical control over their bladder muscles anywhere from 18 months to 3 years, with 2½ years as the average. If you consistently find your twins with dry diapers in the morning or after a nap, or they don't urinate for several hours during the day, they're probably physically ready for the potty. But children must be mentally mature as well. If they begin to ask about the toilet and show an interest in using it, chances are they are ready to begin. While many twins are primed to train at the same time, many more are not; especially boy-girl twins, where the difference can be six months or longer.

Separately or Together?

We trained them at the same time. One of them seemed to be more ready and interested, which in turn caused the other to feel compelled to follow suit out of fear of her sister being able to do something she couldn't. It was almost like a competitive spirit that seemed to motivate her, and it worked.

Training your twins separately, some parents find, is less confusing, with fewer accidents to deal with, but it takes longer. Therefore, most parents wait until both twins show readiness signs and train their twins together. If one twin is ready to train before the other, parents wait for the unready twin to catch up.

Training twins together has many benefits.

- When one twin walks off to use the potty, the other usually follows.

- Competitive twins usually learn more quickly than the average child.

- The overall process takes less time than training them separately.

- Same-sex twins learn from each other through imitation.

Tips for Successful Toilet Training

- From an early age, allow your twins to watch you or an older sibling use the toilet—kids love to imitate.

- Take twins to the potty every two hours and make the experience pleasurable by having toys and picture books nearby. Never let them stay on their potty chairs for longer than 15 minutes at a time.

- Never push children into toilet training before they are ready, or encourage competition with unkind reprimands like "Why can't you use the toilet like your brother?"

- Incentives such as colorful stickers, superhero underwear, and high-spirited praise work well, but keep them to a minimum if one twin is having difficulty getting the hang of it and becomes sensitive.

- Keep clothing simple during the process so twins can undress quickly and easily before using the toilet. (Many parents wait until summer and let the kids run around bare bottomed!)

- Have realistic expectations—accidents will happen.

- If you can't decide what to buy—one or two potty chairs or a seat that fits directly over the toilet—parents recommend two potty chairs for younger recruits (they can keep each other company), and one seat to share for older trainees.

In Sickness and in Health

It shouldn't come as a big surprise that when one twin gets sick, the other is soon to follow. That means that even a simple cold could be stretched out for weeks as both children recover. It's useless (not to mention close to impossible) to isolate twins from each other, as most childhood illnesses are contagious at least 24 hours before any symptoms are exhibited. If your duo does get sick at the same time, simplify your life by forgoing their regular schedule. Let them tell you when it's naptime, dinnertime, and bedtime. Simplify your household chores, too. When your kids are well, then you can pull out the vacuum. Until then, spend your time nursing your little ones back to health.

While caring for two sick infants or toddlers at once is very stressful, tending to one patient while the healthy twin stands by can take its toll on you, too. The well child often loudly exhibits frustration with the situation, simply because he or she doesn't understand why the co-twin is getting all the attention while he or she is getting none. Allowing the healthy child to help take care of the ill twin can help to alleviate much of the whining. Simple tasks like delivering lunch or retrieving an additional blanket helps the healthy one feel needed and important.

Although illnesses are a major part of growing up, there are ways to keep everyone healthier, cutting down on the severity of the illness.

- Encourage hand washing before and after eating, after using the toilet, and after your children blow their noses.

- Assign everyone in the household a personal toothbrush, washcloth, and hand and bath towels, and discourage sharing. Use paper towels instead of cloth in the kitchen.

- Wash toys regularly with warm soapy water, especially if the kids love to put them in their mouths. Clean high-traffic areas such as stair railings, telephones, and countertops regularly with a weak bleach solution.

- Make sure everyone gets enough rest and eats a balanced diet.

One More Pair?

The toddler years are a time of contradictions. On the one hand, "double trouble," however tired that expression has become, aptly describes preschool twins. From the moment they learn the words *no* and *mine*, they'll test your patience on a daily basis. Yet it's also a delightful period. As your twins' special friendship with each other grows and they become active participants in the family, you'll find yourself secretly wishing for an additional set.

·8·

School Days

We saw a huge difference in their interests and personalities since they were 2½ years old. Since that time they've been in separate preschool classes and will be separated in kindergarten. This has helped me out greatly as I can now see who needs work in which areas. Daniel has always been in his brother's shadow and needs to be more on his own. Time away from each other during the day helps them develop their own skills, interests, friends, self-confidence, and self-esteem. I have no problem with separating since they see each other all the time at home and on weekends.

Developmental Milestones

When they were infants, your twins made enormous strides both physically and mentally. As if by magic, they transformed right before your eyes, adding a new word or motor skill daily. Now that they've reached their school years, their developmental milestones are less pronounced but continue to be important nonetheless. It's during ages five to seven that children, especially twins, learn about their world outside their home as they spend more hours away from their parents and each other.

Enrolling in kindergarten is the high point for any five-year-old child. The beginning of school means that five-year-old is growing up, developing more independence, making new friends, and—possibly for the first time—parting company with his or her twin. Five-year-olds still enjoy alone time where they can set the rules of the game, but they're learning more about cooperation and can easily interact with a group of children. Most twins have an easier time socializing within a peer group. After all, they are masters at cooperation and taking turns. It's a talent they had to learn straight from the womb. They work well together solving puzzles and playing board games. Cooperation begins at home, though, where many twins help each other dress in the morning, patiently taking turns with clumsy buttons and snaps.

Morality comes into play at this age, too, as your twins begin to understand the difference between right and wrong. Yet sometimes they might take things a little too far. Many doppelgängers will "take the fall" for their twins—a sensitive sibling will often confess to a crime he or she didn't commit just so the other won't be punished. However, the opposite is also true as many a twin takes guilty pleasure in watching the co-twin take the rap for a crime he or she committed.

As their sixth birthday approaches, your twins are focused more on their new friendships and dealing with outside relationships than with family members. They look more to their friends than to Mom and Dad to answer their questions. Opinions matter. And while peer pressure may not seem like an ideal way for any child to learn about life, relax. Children who imitate are simply learning to live in a larger society, trying to understand their position in life and how they fit into the big scheme of things. Feeling that they belong to a group actually helps them build self-esteem. Yet sometimes fragile twin egos get bruised at this age, especially if an independent twin has the need to break away from a more dependent sibling.

By age seven, children are ready for household chores as they take pleasure in completing a task. Their attention span has lengthened to a point where they actually will finish the project at hand. But give twins separate chores to complete—it cuts down on intratwin fighting and helps them to develop their own individualities as well as learn how to work independently. Physically, watch your twins' balance take hold as they learn to ride bikes. And it's also about this time that your kids will lose their very first baby teeth—a big milestone indeed.

The Great Debate: Should You Put Your Twins in the Same Classroom?

Up until a few months ago I was ready to fight the fight to keep my twins together for kindergarten this fall. I had no intention of separating them even though my son kept telling me he didn't want to be in class with Taylor. Then I had a conference with their preschool teachers who told me that it would be in my twins' best interest to separate them. As much as I believe it's up to the parents to make the decision, we have to trust that their teachers have a better idea of how they'll handle themselves in the classroom. The teachers felt that although they love each other, Jackson would be happier with Taylor if they didn't spend so much time together. I didn't agree at first, but then I started to observe him and watch them together. He told me he'd like her more if he was in his own class. I have decided to separate them.

At this age, the most important twin-specific issue facing parents of multiples involves enrolling their duo in school. Should parents put their twins in the same class, or should they separate them? Some school districts allow parents to decide which is best for their particular family (many states have recently passed laws guaranteeing parents the right to decide) while others have strict policies mandating sibling separation regardless of the situation. Before we get into what the research shows (and doesn't show), let's review some basic advantages to each.

Advantages of Placing Both in the Same Class

- Twins usually adjust to school life more quickly when placed in the same class. Parents say this is a tremendous help if one twin is shy or if neither attended preschool. And for twins who have been inseparable for the last five years, it may be too harsh to abruptly divide the pair.

  My twins just completed kindergarten together. I decided it was best since they had no other school experience and they were going through several major life changes—their grandfather had passed away, I was pregnant with our third baby, and we were moving to a new house—so I felt separating them would be too much.

- Twins have an instant friend and lunch buddy. They support each other, offering reassurance and encouragement. They rarely feel left out.

- Once the initial adjustment period is over, twins won't spend much time together, but they take comfort in knowing that they are in the same room.

Connor and Evan have done well together this year. They both participate in class. They have different friends and share some friends. They sit at different tables and have no problem with that. They would like to be placed together next year, but we've been considering splitting them for first grade. I suspect they may actually flourish even more when separated. Although they have excellent behavior at school, they sometimes misbehave at home. I thought by splitting them next year, they would appreciate seeing each other more when they come home, and hopefully behave better.

- It's more convenient. If there are only two kindergarten sessions, one in the morning and one in the afternoon, many parents don't relish the thought of driving to school four times a day or scheduling additional day care. It's easier too with only one class party, one field trip, one teacher, and one type of homework assignment. (Although parents need to let each twin complete his or her assignment separately as it helps the teacher identify academic strengths as well as areas that need assistance.) Unless there's a problem that warrants separation, parents say, why bother?

Advantages of Placing Both in Separate Classes

- Competitive twins fare better in separate classes, where they are free to progress at their own pace especially if their learning styles or abilities are vastly different.

- Twins who are experiencing language delay may also do better in separate classes, where they are forced to speak for themselves as well as have an opportunity to imitate the correct speech of others around them.

I had always intended to keep Michael and Kyle together until they wanted to be separated, but recently my thinking has changed and we're planning on separating them for first grade. One will answer for the other if the other doesn't answer fast enough, which is fine with the other as it gets him "off the hook"! We discovered this during homework and now have to do it separately with each child. Their teacher confirmed this was happening, and she suggested separating them. One is OK with it; the other isn't. We've started to prepare them for next fall.

- Sometimes twins who are placed in the same class keep to themselves, rarely interacting with the other children, and subsequently have a more difficult time making new friends. In addition, "tough-guy" twins can band together and be disruptive.

- Identical twins who are often mistaken for the other benefit greatly when placed in separate classes, where teachers and students won't confuse or compare the pair.

- It gives each child an opportunity to experience life on his or her own as twins usually spend 24/7 with each other. Some children become resentful at having to share everything, including a classroom. Children who are separated, on the other hand, are excited to see each other at the end of the day to share unique stories about their separate lives.

What the Research Tells Us

Local school districts continue to knock heads with parents who want to keep their multiples together in class. In fact, it's the number one source of conflict between parents of twins and school administrators. The bone of contention centers on individuality—if twins are placed together, school principals argue, they'll have a much harder time forming their autonomy. Parents, on the other hand, have a variety of reasons for wishing to keep their children together, and they insist they know their children best. Therefore, parents argue, they should have the final say. But what does the research show?

Placing twins together has benefits (one study found Dutch twins sharing a classroom had higher reading and math scores than those in separate classrooms), but separating twins also has rewards (twins can progress at their own pace without comparisons to a co-twin). Ironically, counter to what many school boards, superintendents, and administrators may think, there's no empirical evidence that sharing a classroom is harmful to twins' development (except for very rare and severely pathological cases). In fact, some twins suffer when separated. For instance, a longitudinal study done in the United Kingdom and published in 2004 looked at the effect classroom separation had on twins' behavior, school progress, and reading abilities. Researchers assessed approximately 1,800 same-sex, identical and nonidentical twins at two different times—during the first year of school at age five and then 18 months later at age seven. Three groups of twins were examined—those who were together in class the first year and then stayed together the second year; twins who were separated the first and second year; and finally, children who were together the first year and then separated the second year.

The results showed that the two groups who were separated exhibited more internalizing problems (anxiety, depression, and withdrawal) than the group who was never separated. Monozygotic twins suffered more than nonidentical twins. Furthermore, internalizing problems actually increased with children who were separated the second year. Additionally, they also scored lower on reading tests. The study, however, showed that same-sex, nonidentical twins who were separated the second year were actually rated as working harder in class than their counterparts who were not separated.

Obviously not all twins who are separated in the beginning of school or in the year following will suffer, but it does illuminate the need for school administrators to adopt a more flexible policy as some multiples just deal better with separation than others.

How to Choose What's Best for Your Kids

All the parents I surveyed took a very thoughtful approach when considering the issue. And this is key to a happy outcome. Parents must take themselves out of the equation (don't worry, separation won't destroy the twin bond) and instead look at their children's relationship to each other and individually. For instance, what kind of bond do they have? Are they tightly connected, or are they comfortable being away from one another? Are they social and enjoy meeting other children? Do they compete for attention or for academic accolades? Are they vastly different in abilities and/or temperament? Is one thoughtful and sensitive; the other impulsive and outgoing? Does one "mother" or constantly do for the other? Is one child always in the shadow of his or her co-twin? All these factors are important and need to be considered.

If your children are to be in separate classes and up until this point haven't spent much time apart, it is wise to slowly begin acclimating them well before the first day of school. One way to begin this process is to run errands with just one child, leaving the sibling home with another parent, or have each child spend the night at Grandma's house separately. Another possibility is to enroll each child in a different sport or club so each gets a taste of "doing his own thing."

Remember, too, what may work one year for your twins may be totally wrong for them the following year. Therefore, be sure to reevaluate their needs at the end of each school year by discussing your options with your children's teacher and adjust your future plans accordingly.

But what if your school district's policy goes against your wishes? Many local twins' clubs and families are fighting back and lobbying their state representatives. Several states have been successful in passing laws that give parents the final say in their children's classroom placement. To see if your state is one of them or to join in the fight, log on to Twins Law (twinslaw.com).

Twins and Friends

As toddlers, twins are inseparable, always seeking out each other's company, but once school begins, it's inevitable that the pair will separate and experience unique events of their own. And separate friends should be a part of the mix. It's important for children's developing self-esteem to form separate relationships. When twins play with "outsiders," it promotes proper speech development, boosts their confidence, and cultivates social skills that they'll need for the future. In effect, it readies them for the real world.

For close-knit twins, especially monozygotic twins, making new friends can be difficult. A twin may be reluctant to continue socializing with a new playmate who doesn't do things the way his or her twin does. And while a singleton is forced to make friends out of loneliness, twins are not—they have each other as playmates. Encourage interac-

TOP FIVE BIRTHDAY PARTY NO-NOS

When twins are young, they hardly notice their birthdays. Once they reach school age, however, just like every other red-blooded kid, birthdays become important. So how do parents give twins what each wants, short of planning two separate parties? As one mom solemnly noted, "They don't want to share much else, but they know that they have to share a birthday." With a little imagination, parents can pull off a successful party where each twin will feel special. But before you rent a clown, consider these no-nos.

1. **One cake; one song.** Every child deserves to be in the birthday spotlight alone (even if it is only for a few minutes). Let each child choose a favorite cake (cakes don't have to be big; two small cakes will suffice) and then sing "Happy Birthday" twice—once for each child. But who gets sung to first? Alternate years, and don't worry—they'll remember whose turn it is.

2. **The shared gift faux pas.** By now, parents know that they should give each child his or her own special gift, but how do you delicately get the message out to well-meaning party guests who consistently show up with one toy for the twins to share? One mom handled this touchy situation by writing a poem and including it in each invitation:

   If you're thinking of a special gift,
   Let us help you with a clue.
   We like just about anything,
   Just as long as there are two!

3. **One guest list.** Insisting that your twins agree on the guest list is not only unfair but sure to start an argument. So how do you avoid a crowd of children on the day of the party? First, decide on the guest count (it helps to make it an even number); then divide it in half and allow each child to choose his or her own guests.

4. **Playing up twin status.** Presenting the "birthday twins" as a unit by dressing them alike on their special day erroneously reinforces to family and friends that the two are actually one. Encourage each child to choose his or her own special birthday outfit.

5. **Identical kids, identical gifts.** Party guests, afraid to show favoritism, sometimes show up with two identical gifts. While not always a problem, especially for young twins, older twins may not appreciate the gesture. Once again, a simple note on the invitation can do the trick: "Jake's passion of the year: dinosaurs. Tom's passion of the year: airplanes."

• •

tive play between your twins and their cousins, neighbors, or play group buddies. From an early age, take your twosome to the park for weekly play groups. The longer you take to introduce your twins to other children, the more difficult the process of making new friends becomes.

When arranging play dates for preschool twins, however, it's wise to invite two friends over to play rather than just one. If only one child is present, twins may either gang up on that child (and that's the end of that friendship!) or one twin may take the child under his or her wing, excluding the co-twin. Having two playmates evens the playing field—each child can pick a buddy and break off into a smaller group as children often do.

As you nurture your twins' outside friendships, sooner or later exclusion occurs when one receives an invitation that the other does not. How your left-out child reacts will depend greatly on how you react. It's unfair to think that if one twin is asked somewhere that the other twin should be included, too. Although you may be just trying to ease hurt feelings, others may view your twins as an "all or nothing" proposition and not invite your twins again in the future. Instead, if one twin gets invited to a birthday party and the other doesn't, make special plans to go to the zoo or park with the excluded sibling.

TIPS TO ENCOURAGE OUTSIDE RELATIONSHIPS

- Early in twins' toddler years, join a neighborhood play group and seek out same-aged playmates. A great place to start is your local twins group—they often organize weekly play dates at local parks.

- Encourage (but never force) twins to make separate friends by allowing your children to invite playmates over after school or on weekends.

- If possible, enroll twins in separate preschool classes, pee-wee sports programs, or even art classes.

Twins Asserting Their Independence

The need for twins to be different from one another by pulling away from their special relationship is a natural step in growing up and developing a sense of self. Some school-aged twins see their twinship as an asset, others a liability. Psychologists say that intratwin fighting is not only normal at this age, but it is needed in an effort for each child to form his or her own individuality.

Twins have a doubly hard time in their quests to become individuals. As infants, all children see themselves as part of their caretaker, or mother. But as they get older, they slowly understand their sense of self and ultimately form their own identities. Twins, on the other hand, must separate not only from their mother but also from each other. Compounding the situation is the twin bond itself—an intense relationship that exceeds the closeness of two different-aged siblings. While twins want to individualize, they sometimes feel guilt at the prospect of separating from their twin, someone they truly love.

For some twins, especially identical twins, the process of breaking away is difficult. When similar-looking twins gaze into a mirror, whose reflection do they see? Their own or their twin's? Are they one person or two? Many young twins having trouble forming identities, often using singular verbs when referring to themselves as a group: "I went to the store with Mommy," or when asked their names, they might answer using both, "My name is Kevin-Jeff."

While these problems eventually correct themselves, parents can help their twins evolve their identities from an early age by following these guidelines.

- Treat each twin as an individual by choosing different-sounding names and dressing each in different-style clothing. Address each child individually rather than speaking to them as a group.

- If possible, give each twin his or her own room, or at least a personal space for toys and other possessions.

- Starting when your twins are young, give each a mirror. Point to each reflection and repeat the name.

- Tap into their interests and encourage them to pursue individual hobbies.

- Carve out one-on-one time each and every day through snuggling, reading, and cooking.

The Need to Compare and Contrast Twins

It happens as early as the first day while they're still in the hospital: Baby A weighs more than Baby B; Baby A is taller than Baby B. Parents naturally compare their new arrivals, looking for similarities as well as differences. Even if they never compared their other children of different ages, parents of twins now feel the need to distinguish one twin from the other. Solely because of their twinship, everyone—from family to strangers—compares one twin to the other and says things to twins that an adult would never think of saying to two siblings of different ages. "Which one of you is smarter?" is often a favorite.

While there is nothing inherently wrong with comparing twins (in fact, it's quite normal), constantly contrasting older twins often leads to intratwin competition and rivalry. The pair will compete in school and sports, and even worse, they'll vie for parental attention. It can also lead to the appearance of favoritism when one twin's trait is praised, giving the impression of superiority over the co-twin. This can be damaging to fragile egos and self-esteem.

Identical twins survive the compare/contrast dilemma a little easier since they often begin on a level playing field—they're usually both physically and mentally alike. But fraternal twins, who are no more alike than any two siblings reared together, are unfairly compared. Inevitably, one will always be better at something than the other, and they are often reminded of it on a consistent basis. Even parents who object to outsiders comparing their twins sometimes in their quest to instill individuality in their children do it, too. "John is the athlete of the family while Susan is our straight-A student."

THE PITFALLS OF LABELING

As soon as I introduced my twins to the world, the world immediately greeted each of my babies with a label: "Oh, you're the happy one, aren't you? And you, you're the shy one, right?" While these well-meaning people were merely trying to be friendly, their comments baffled me. How can they possibly make such a quick judgment, I thought. They don't even know my kids! Placing labels on twins is a common practice as family, friends, and even strangers struggle to differentiate one twin from the other. While comparing is natural, labeling is dangerous, inhibiting twins' growth and development.

When parents classify each child daily with comments like, "Joan's the musical one, and Tom's the bookworm," twins hear these comments, internalize them, and soon believe them. In effect, Mom and Dad have branded their twins. Through a self-fulfilling prophecy, it becomes a part of them. ("Well, if they said it, it must be true. I'm not the musical one, Joan is.") The result of these innocent comments is that children sometimes don't reach their full potential. If a child thinks that his or her twin has an edge on a specific talent, that child may step back and never try to achieve greatness in the same area. Comparing is normal, but labeling is too rigid and doesn't permit change. It inhibits development.

PLAYING FAVORITES

Although they hate to admit it, many parents do have favorites when it comes to their twins—it just depends on the day of the week.

Top Five Ways to Avoid Unhealthy Competition Between Twins

While competition can help spur many twins to achieve great goals, too much can hurt the twin bond and disrupt an otherwise harmonious family. Walking the fine line between spirited competition and unhealthy rivalry is shaky, but parents can help their twins to take off their boxing gloves by following these tips.

1. **Build on each child's individual strengths.** Focus more on the effort—and praise it—rather than the outcome. ("I can tell you were really trying your best. Good job!")

2. **Reaffirm parental love.** From the first day, twins compete for attention. Remind your children often that there's plenty of love to go around. "Mom and Dad love both of you individually and uniquely. You don't need to compete for our love. You already have it."

3. **Remind them that all things are not created equal.** They may share a birthday, but twins need to realize that life is not always equal. Someone will always be better at something. Then shrug it off.

4. **Don't fuel the fire.** Catch yourself when you inadvertently compare each child's abilities against the other's. Advise family and friends if they do the same.

5. **Avoid the firstborn rank.** Unless your family is part of British royalty, where the next in line for the throne will not be in dispute, don't refer to your twins as "the younger" or "the older." Stressing birth order only intensifies twin rivalry.

Why It Happens

It's human nature to feel closer to one child than another. Unlike animals, humans bond with one offspring at a time. And when two infants suddenly appear in the picture, parents feel guilty when they don't have similar feelings for both. Favoritism can begin as far back as the day the twins are born. Parents of newborn twins, fresh from the hospital, report feeling closer to the more responsive twin, or the less fussy of the two, or in the case of premature twins, the one who is released from the hospital first, or the sicker twin still recovering in the neonatal intensive care unit and in need of more attention. But, most parents say, these are only temporary feelings, and within weeks, their love for both deepens.

But what if they're not temporary feelings? What if your feelings for one twin never catch up and you find yourself drawn to one baby more than the other? All children have distinct temperaments and different rates of development. Some children are more difficult to be around; it's only natural to find yourself not wanting to be in this twin's company.

Tips on Overcoming Favoritism

- Admit to yourself that you have a favorite and acknowledge that it's a normal feeling.

- Focus on the traits you do enjoy in the unfavored child.

- Find common interests and hobbies with the unfavored child, and then do them together.

- Help the unfavored child improve unfavorable behavior. For instance, give the whiner an alternative way to ask for what he or she wants.

But That's Not Fair!

Some double-duty parents take the "both or neither" approach when dealing with issues of fairness. If one twin needs a new pair of gym shoes, both get a pair. Or if only one child wants to go to summer camp, then neither attends, or the child that doesn't attend gets to do something special (in other words, expensive) to keep things "even." Families admit this approach prevents feuding and bad feelings between twins, but it's costly.

Many parents give each twin the exact same item out of guilt or fear of showing favoritism. And it doesn't take long for twins to pick up on this, manipulating the situation to their advantage. Children whose parents take this approach keep a mental tally of who got what when and remind parents on a daily basis. They learn early on that Mom or Dad can be coerced into giving.

With twins, it's easy to become overly concerned with trying to be fair, but like all things in life, nothing is ever equal. Moreover, trying to keep things equal all the time is an impossible task. What if one child needs money for college and the other has received a scholarship? Just to be fair, will you feel compelled to give the scholar the same amount of money as the child in need?

From early childhood, concern yourself with giving each child what he or she needs by responding to that child individually. Give because of need or love, not because of appeasement or guilt.

Twins as Adolescents and Adults

As parents watch their twins grow, they often worry about the intratwin relationship more than they would about the connection between any two siblings. Are the twins too dependent on each other, they ask? Are they too distant with nothing in common? How twins relate to each other as adults largely depends on how they weather that enchanting period of life called adolescence. When twins teeter precariously between childhood and adulthood, intratwin rivalry and jealousy are heightened as the two fight for their independence.

The teen years cause the greatest stress on families with twins. With increased peer pressure and the need to explore and experiment, not only does the pair break away from parental control, but the twins often deny their twinship as well. It can become even more disruptive if one twin matures faster both physically and emotionally than the other. Resentment may build if, for instance, parents feel one twin is more mature and ready to date while the other isn't. Do parents deny both twins the privilege when they wouldn't if the mature child were a singleton? A private, heart-to-heart talk with the less mature teen explaining that the decision to deny dating is only temporary will help mend hurt feelings more quickly.

Older children still need boundaries, and parents need to set limits and be consistent in enforcing them. If the teens help formulate house rules, however, they are less likely to break them.

The need for privacy also increases during this period. Many same-sex teenage twins are relentless in their quest for their own rooms. Parents who aren't able to accommodate their children's insistent wishes can increase privacy by adding a room divider to the twins' bedroom or offering each a separate closet or dresser. You might want to remind them that learning to share a room successfully is a good lesson since much of adult life is spent sharing.

While some twins may temporarily deny their twinship during adolescence, others become closer, taking solace in their bond. They might feel that no one understands them better than their twin. Unfortunately, these twins can unite against parents, fanning the generation-gap flames.

Whether your twins become inseparable buddies or mortal enemies, as any parent with grown children will tell you, during the teen years you're in for a bumpy ride. Don't forget to fasten your seat belts.

By the time they reach adulthood, most twins who have adamantly denied their twinship usually rekindle their relationship. Adolescence isn't the only marker for the type of relationship that they'll have as adults; twin type plays an important role as well. Identical female twins usually remain the closest out of all twin types, followed by identical males. This is not surprising since most identical twins are closer during childhood and share many of the same interests (not to mention DNA). Fraternal female twins are often closer than most singleton sisters, as are fraternal male twins, but much depends on how close they live to each other. While adult male-female twins are the least close of twin pairs, they are usually more connected than most male-female siblings—but their bond is due in large part to the effort (or lack thereof) of the female twin.

The Last Word

Who would have ever thought that having twins would be so complicated? Well, actually it isn't. Your mind may be reeling from all the information that you've just ingested, but relax—you already know plenty about parenting twins. Just follow your heart, and indulge me one last time with a few favorite clichés.

This Too Shall Pass

Whether it's from lack of sleep or just trying to adjust to your new life, the first year with new twins is definitely the hardest. But before you know it, your twins will be running around the house and you'll be missing the days when they were portable infants and you could hug them whenever you wanted. (Now you have to try to catch them first!) With this in mind, remember: When they start to throw the cat food around your kitchen, breathe deeply and repeat, "This too shall pass."

The Grass Is Always Greener on the Other Side of the Fence

With twins, there's never enough time to give each child that special one-on-one time. As you look at other parents cooing over their only child, it's easy to sigh to yourself and feel slightly envious. I have felt that way, and on those occasions when I wonder about a different life, the feeling doesn't last long. My boys pull me back to my reality with their devilish smiles and wet kisses, and I think to myself that I must have done something extraordinary in a past life to have been so blessed.

Go with Your Gut

I've tried to give you various perspectives on the unique problems parents face raising twins—dress them alike, don't dress them alike; separate them for the day, don't separate them; put them in the same class, don't put them in the same class; and so on. But all these decisions can be confusing, not to mention overwhelming, for new parents. Am I doing the right thing, you ask? Will I hurt my children's self-esteem if I choose one way over another? While I encourage you to use this book as a guide, it's more important to listen to your heart and do what you think is best for your twins. Only you know what each of your children needs. Trust your instincts. They won't steer you wrong.

Appendix

Suggested Reading and Bibliography

Al-Najashi, S. S., and A. A. Al-Mulhim. "Prolongation of Pregnancy in Multiple Pregnancy." *International Journal of Gynecology and Obstetrics* 54 (1996): 131–135.

Antsaklis, A. "Management of the Twin-to-Twin Transfusion Syndrome." *The Ultrasound Review of Obstetrics and Gynecology* 5 (2005): 75–80.

Arabin, B., and J. van Eyck. "Role of Ultrasound in Multiple Pregnancy." *Twin Research* 4 (2001): 141–145.

Bacon, K. " 'It's Good to Be Different': Parent and Child Negotiations of 'Twin' Identity." *Twin Research and Human Genetics* 9 (2006): 141–147.

Bakalar, N. "Rise in Rate of Twin Births May Be Tied to the Dairy Case." *New York Times* (May 30, 2006).

Blickstein, I., and R. B. Kalish. "Birth Discordance in Multiple Pregnancy." *Twin Research* 6 (2003): 526–531.

Bouchard, T. J., D. T. Lykken, M. McGue, et al. "Sources of Human Psychological Differences: The Minnesota Study of Twins Reared Apart." *Science* 250 (1990): 223–229.

Brewer, G. S., and T. Brewer. *What Every Pregnant Woman Should Know: The Truth About Diet and Drugs in Pregnancy*, rev. ed. Baltimore: Penguin Books, 1985.

Catt, J., T. Wood, M. Henman, et al. "Single Embryo Transfer in IVF to Prevent Multiple Pregnancy." *Twins Research* 6 (2003): 536–539.

Crowther, C. A. "Bed Rest in Hospital for Multiple Pregnancy." *Birth* 26 (1999): 201–202.

De Catte, L., I. Liebaers, and W. Foulon. "Outcome of Twin Gestations After First Trimester Chorionic Villus Sampling." *Obstetrics and Gynecology* 96 (2000): 714–720.

Dominus, S. "For an Era of Twins, the End May Be Near." *New York Times* (February 11, 2008).

Eriksson, A. W., and J. Fellman. "Seasonal Variations of Live Births, Stillbirths, Extramarital Births and Twin Maternities in Switzerland." *Twin Research* 3 (2000): 189–201.

Ferrari, R. M., M. A. Cooney, A. Vexler, et al. "Time to Pregnancy and Multiple Births." *Human Reproduction* 22 (2007): 407–413.

Fisher, J., and A. Stocky. "Maternal Perinatal Mental Health and Multiple Births: Implications for Practice." *Twin Research* 6 (2003): 506–513.

Forget-Dubois, N., D. Perusse, G. Turecki, et al. "Diagnosing Zygosity in Infant Twins: Physical Similarity, Genotyping, and Chorionicity." *Twin Research* 6 (2003): 479–485.

Gao, W., L. Li, W. Cao, et al. "Determination of Zygosity by Questionnaire and Physical Features Comparison in Chinese Adult

Twins." *Twin Research and Human Genetics* 9 (2006): 266–271.

Garitte, C., J. P. Almodovar, E. Benjamin, et al. "Speech in Same- and Different-Sex Twins 4 and 5 Years Old." *Twin Research* 5 (2002): 538–543.

Geraghty, S., J. Khoury, and H. Kalkwarf. "Comparison of Feeding Among Multiple Birth Infants." *Twin Research* 7 (2004): 542–547.

Gilkerson, J., and J. Richards. *The Power of Talk: Adult Talk and Conversational Turns During the Critical 0–3 Years of Child Development.* Boulder, CO: Infoture, Inc. (2007).

Gray, P. H., R. Cincotta, F. Y. Chan, et al. "Perinatal Outcomes with Laser Surgery for Twin-Twin Transfusion Syndrome." *Twin Research and Human Genetics* 9 (2006): 438–443.

Haram, K., E. Svendsen, and O. Myking. "Growth Restriction: Etiology, Maternal and Neonatal Outcome. A Review." *Current Women's Health Reviews* 3 (2007): 145–160.

Harlaar, N., M. Hayiou-Thomas, P. Dale, et al. "Why Do Preschool Language Abilities Correlate with Later Reading? A Twin Study." *Journal of Speech, Language, and Hearing Research* 51 (2008): 688–705.

Hata, T., S. Aoki, K. Miyazaki, et al. "Three Dimensional Ultrasonographic Visualization of Multiple Pregnancy." *Gynecologic and Obstetric Investigation* 46 (1998): 26–30.

Hay, D. A. "Together or Apart?" *Twin Research* 7 (2004): iii–iv.

Hayashi, C., K. Hayakawa, C. Tsuboi, et al. "Relationship Between Parents' Report Rate of Twin Language and Factors Related to Linguistic Development: Older Sibling, Nonverbal Play and Preschool Attendance." *Twin Research and Human Genetics* 9 (2006): 165–174.

Heh, S., L. Huang, S. Ho, et al. "Effectiveness of an Exercise Support Program in Reducing the Severity of Postnatal Depression in Taiwanese Women." *Birth* 35 (2008): 60–65.

Knight, M. "Eclampsia in the United Kingdom 2005." *BJOG: An International Journal of Obstetrics & Gynaecology* 114 (2007): 1072–1078.

Koch, H. L. *Twins and Twin Relations.* Chicago: The University of Chicago Press, 1966.

Luke, B., S. J. Min, B. Gillespie, et al. "The Importance of Early Weight Gain in the Intrauterine Growth and Birthweight of Twins." *American Journal of Obstetrics and Gynecology* 179 (1998): 1155–1161.

Machado, R. C. A., M. L. Brizot, A. W. Liao, et al. "Prenatal Sonographic Prediction of Twin Growth Discordance." *Twin Research and Human Genetics* 10 (2007): 198–201.

Maconochie, N., P. Doyle, S. Prior, et al. "Risk Factors for First Trimester Miscarriage: Results from a UK-Based-Population Case-Control Study." *BJOG: An International Journal of Obstetrics & Gynaecology* 114 (2007): 170–186.

Martin, J. A., B. E. Hamilton, P. D. Sutton, et al. "Births: Final Data for 2005." *National Vital Statistics Report* 56 (2007): 1–104.

McEwen, F., F. Happe, P. Bolton, et al. "Origins of Individual Differences in Imitation: Links with Language, Pretend Play, and Socially Insightful Behavior in Two-Year-Old Twins." *Child Development* 78 (2007): 474–492.

Nicolaides, K. H., N. J. Sebire, R. Snijders, et al. *The 11–14 Weeks Scan* (ISUOG Educational Series). Campinas: Centrus, 2001.

O'Connor, A. "The Claim: Identical Twins Have Identical Fingerprints." *New York Times* (November 2, 2004).

Piontelli, A. *Twins: From Fetus to Child.* London: Routledge, 2002.

Piontelli, A., L. Bocconi, C. Boschetto, et al. "Differences and Similarities in the Intra-Uterine Behaviour of Monozygotic and Dizygotic Twins." *Twin Research* 2 (1999): 264–273.

Pison, G., and A. V. D'Addato. "Frequency of Twin Births in Developed Countries." *Twin Research and Human Genetics* 9 (2006): 250–259.

Price, T. S., B. Freeman, I. Craig, et al. "Infant Zygosity Can Be Assigned by Parental Report Questionnaire Data." *Twin Research* 3 (2000): 129–133.

Rietveld, M. J. H., J. C. van der Valk, I. L. Bongers, et al. "Zygosity Diagnosis in Young Twins by Parental Report." *Twin Research* 3 (2000): 134–141.

Roem, K. "Nutritional Management of Multiple Pregnancy." *Twin Research* 6 (2003): 514–519.

Sandbank, A. C. *Twin and Triplet Psychology: A Professional Guide to Working with Multiples.* London: Routledge, 1999.

Scheinfeld, A. *Twins and Supertwins.* Philadelphia: J. B. Lippincott Company, 1967.

Shapiro, J. L., R. Kung, and J. F. R. Barrett. "Cervical Length as a Predictor of Pre-Term Birth in Twin Gestations." *Twin Research* 3 (2000): 213–216.

Sherer, D. M., M. L. D'Amico, C. Cox, et al. "Association of In Utero Behavioral Patterns of Twins with Each Other as Indicated by Fetal Heart Rate Reactivity and Nonreactivity." *American Journal of Perinatology* 3 (1994): 208–212.

Smith, G. N., M. C. Walker, A. Ohlsson, et al. "Randomized Double-Blind Placebo-Controlled Trial of Transdermal Nitroglycerin for Preterm Labor." *American Journal of Obstetrics and Gynecology* 62 (2007): 358–360.

Souter, V., M. A. Parisi, D. R. Nyholt, et al. "A Case of True Hermaphroditism Reveals an Unusual Mechanism of Twinning." *Human Genetics* 121 (2007): 179–185.

Sueters, M., J. M. Middeldorp, E. Lopriore, et al. "Timely Diagnosis of Twin-to-Twin Transfusion Syndrome in Monochorionic Twin Pregnancies by Biweekly Sonography Combined with Patient Instruction to Report Onset of Symptoms." *Ultrasound in Obstetrics and Gynecology* 28 (2006): 659–664.

Tarkan, L. "Lowering Odds of Multiple Births." *New York Times* (February 19, 2008).

Tinglof, C. B. *Parenting School-Age Twins and Multiples.* New York: McGraw-Hill, 2007.

Toledo, M. G. "Is There Increased Monozygotic Twinning After Assisted Reproductive Technology?" *Australian and New Zealand Journal of Obstetrics and Gynaecology* 45 (2005): 360–364.

Tully, L. A., T. E. Moffitt, A. Caspi, et al. "What Effect Does Classroom Separation Have on Twins' Behavior, Progress at School, and Reading Abilities?" *Twin Research* 7 (2004): 115–124.

Webbink, D., D. Hay, and P. M. Visscher. "Does Sharing the Same Class in School Improve Cognitive Abilities of Twins?" *Twin Research and Human Genetics* 10 (2007): 573–580.

Yukobowich, E., E. Y. Anteby, S. M. Cohen, et al. "Risk of Fetal Loss in Twin Pregnancies Undergoing Second Trimester Amniocentesis." *Obstetrics and Gynecology* 98 (2001): 231–234.

Twin Resources and Websites

Talk About Twins (talk-about-twins.com)
Devoted to twins, twin relationships, and parenting twins, this website covers the latest news in twin pregnancy, twin bond, school-age twins, and traveling with twins. See the 16-minute movie, *The Great Debate: Multiples and Classroom Placement.*

Twins magazine (twinsmagazine.com)
Bimonthly periodical on having, parenting, and enjoying twins. The online message boards are very popular. Call toll-free to subscribe: 1-800-558-9467.

About.com: Twins & Multiples (multiples.about.com)
Comprehensive website with articles on twins, photo galleries, and e-mail newsletters to keep you informed on the latest in twinning.

Twins Today (twinstoday.com)
Part of the iParenting network.

Twins and Multiples.org (twinsandmultiples.org)
Dedicated to educating twins, triplets, and more. A great website produced by Pat Preedy and David Hay (one of the foremost twin researchers and the author of the foreword in my book, *Parenting School-Age Twins and Multiples.*)

Twins Days (twinsdays.org)
The official website of the Twins Days Festival held each August in Twinsburg, Ohio.

Sidelines—National High-Risk Pregnancy Support Network (side lines.org)
A nonprofit organization providing international support for women and their families experiencing complicated pregnancies and premature births.

The Twin-to-Twin Transfusion Syndrome Foundation (tttsfounda
tion.org)
Offers immediate educational, emotional, and financial support for
families after the diagnosis of TTTS.

Twin 2 Twin—United Kingdom's Twin-to-Twin Transfusion Syndrome Association (twin2twin.org.uk)
Comprised of parents, professional caregivers, and research profes-
sionals dedicated to raising the awareness of TTTS, funding research,
and providing care and advice to sufferers.

NATIONAL TWINS CLUBS

National Organization of Mothers of Twins Clubs—NOMOTC
(nomotc.org)
Official website of the National Organization of Mothers of Twins
Clubs, a U.S. support group for parents of twins and higher order
multiples.

Australian Multiple Birth Association—AMBA (amba.org.au)
A nonprofit organization, with more than 66 local groups, that
offers advice and assistance to families with twins, triplets, and
quads.

Irish Multiple Birth Association—IMBA (imba.ie)
Provides support during pregnancy and early childhood years for
parents expecting multiples.

Multiple Births Canada—MBC (multiplebirthscanada.org)
Works to improve the quality of life for families with multiples
through support, education, and a network of local chapters.

Twins and Multiples Birth Association—TAMBA (tamba.org.uk)
An association located in the United Kingdom that provides information and a support network of more than 200 local clubs to parents of multiples.

Free Samples of Baby Products and Coupons

Beechnut Nutrition Corporation
Multiple Birth Program
800-233-2468
Call or log on to beechnut.com to receive a twins promotional packet
of coupons for baby food, as well as information on label-saving
promotions.

Carnation
800-242-5200
Call or log on to verybestbaby.com to register for their Very Best Baby
Resource Center and receive a free *Very Best* magazine as well as
coupons for infant formula and other discounts from participating
partners.

Cottonelle Fresh Flushable Moist Wipes
Log on to cottonelle.com/coupons/aspx for free monthly coupons.

Earth's Best Baby Food
800-442-4221
Call or log on to earthsbest.com for free coupons.

Evenflo Products
Multiple Birth Program
1801 Commerce Dr.
Piqua, OH 45356
800-356-2229
Send copies of babies' birth certificates (blocking out any sensitive
information such as Social Security numbers) to receive free baby
products.

Gerber Products Co.
Gerber Baby Club
800-443-7237
Call for coupons and samples of breastfeeding products, or register
online at gerber.com/register.

Johnson & Johnson Companies
800-526-3967
Call for free New Parents Pack, and log on to baby.com (click on "benefits") for a variety of free Johnson & Johnson baby product coupons.

Kimberly Clark Corporation
Dept. QMB
P.O. Box 2020
Neenah, WI 54957-2020
800-544-1847
Send a copy of babies' birth certificates (blocking out any sensitive information such as Social Security numbers) or log on to Huggiesbabynetwork.com for a one-time supply of diapers and other promotional items.

Lansinoh
800-292-4794
Call for lanolin cream sample.

Procter and Gamble
Pampers Company
Multiple Birth Program
P.O. Box 599
Cincinnati, OH 45201
800-726-7377
Send copy of babies' hospital discharge papers (block out any sensitive information such as Social Security numbers) for a one-time supply of products and coupons.

Ross Laboratories
Welcome Addition Club
800-222-9546
Call for free samples of Similac and Isomil infant formulas.

DNA Test Kits and DNA Labs

Affiliated Genetics
affiliatedgenetics.com
800-362-5559

Beta Paternity
betagenetics.com
800-798-3810

DNA Diagnostics Center
dnacenter.com
800-613-5768

Proactive Genetics
proactivegenetics.com
866-894-6362

Index

•A•

Abruptio placenta, 21
Age of mother, 3
Alcohol, 45–46
Amniocentesis, 15–16
Amniotic sac, 6
Anemia, 20–21
Apnea, 29, 62
Assisted reproductive technology
 (ART), 2–3
Autonomous speech, 146, 156

•B•

Babbling, 146
Baby books, 67

Baby bumpers, 59
Baby carrier, 57
Baby food, 59. *See also* Feeding
 babies
Baby monitor, 55
Baby stations, 77
Baby teeth, losing, 168
Baby wipes, 59–60
Babyproofing, 103, 128–30
Babysitters, 67, 118–20, 121
Bags, 115
Balance, 125
Bathing, 59, 92–93
Bed rest, 26–27, 28
Bedtime, 91–92
Belly support, 38
Bicycle riding, 168
Bill paying, 69

Birth control pills, 3
Birth experience, 61–63
Birth order, 179
Birth plan, 62–63
Birth weight, 29, 38, 39
Birthdays, 174–75
Birthmarks, 6
Blankets, 52, 57, 59
Bleeding, 19
Body language, 47
Body parts, 146
Body temperature, 29
Body type, 4
Bonding
   individual persons, 131–32
   parent-child, 95–99,
      131–32
      for fathers, 98–99
   twin bond, 132, 145–46,
      149–53, 172
Booties, 53
Boppy pillow, 57
Bottle feeding, 85, 87–88
   advantages of, 87
   nighttime feeding,
      89–90
Bottle warmers, 55
Bouchard, Thomas, 153
Bouncer seats. *See* Vibrating
   bouncer seats
Bras, 38
Breast pumps, 84–85
Breastfeeding. *See* Nursing
Business, household, 69
   prioritizing tasks, 76

ᵒ C ᵒ

Caffeine, 45
Calcium, 43
Car seats, 50–51
Cesarean sections, 12, 21–22,
   30
Chairs, hook-on, 114–15
Changing table, 59
Childbirth classes, 62
Chorionic Villus sampling
   (CVS), 16–17
Christmas, 69–70
Climbing, 145
Clomid, 2
Clomiphene citrate, 2
Clothing, 52, 53, 93
   matching outfits, 53
   second-hand, 60–61
Cluster feeding, 91
Cognitive development, 74
Communication, spousal,
   70
Cooing, 154
Cooking, first weeks after
   birth, 63–65
Cooperation skills, 168
Coordination, 103
CPR, 62
Crawling, 103, 125, 126
Creeping, 103, 125
Cribs, 50, 60, 74, 103, 148
   portable, 114–15
Crying, 74
   both babies at once,
      104–5
Cystic fibrosis, 16, 17

·D·

Daddy-and-me play group, 99
Dairy products, 4
Diamniotic-dichorionic pregnancy, 6
Diamniotic-monochorionic pregnancy, 6
Diaper Genie, 55
Diaper services, 69
Diapers, 53–55
  cloth versus disposables, 54
Diet, 4–5, 38–46
  needed calories, 39
Differentiating night and day, 92
Dizygotic twins. *See* Fraternal twins
DNA testing, 7
Do it yourself projects, 59–60
Double stroller, 57
Down syndrome, 17
Dressing and undressing, 92–93, 136–37
Drug intervention, 27, 29
Drugs, illegal, 46

·E·

Edema, 19
Emotions, controlling, 127
Entertainment, 115. *See also* Toys

Environmental factors
  during pregnancy, 4–5
  nature versus nurture theory, 152–153
Equipment, infant, 49–56, 57. *See also specific equipment*
  double-duty items, 59
  one or two items, 49
  second-hand items, 60–61
Equipment, toddler, 56
  double-duty items, 59
  second-hand items, 60–61
Exercises. *See* Physical exercise
Eyesight, 101

·F·

Family and Medical Leave Act, 37
Father. *See* Parenting twins
Fats, 43
Favoritism, 178, 180
Feeding babies, 59, 79–91. *See also* Nursing
  babies feeding themselves, 143–44
  nighttime feedings, 87–92
  solid food, 142–44
Feet, 38
Fertility drugs, 2
  statistics, 2
Fertinex, 2
Fetal alcohol syndrome, 45–46

Fetal complications, 22–24
Fetal heart rates, 150
Fetal limb defects, 17
Finances
    coupons, 60
    day-care centers, 58
    discounts, 60
    do it yourself projects, 59–60
    freebies, 60
    hospital bill, 56–58
    mommy-and-me classes, 58
    preschool, 58
    reevaluating budgets, 58
    second-hand items, 60–61
Fingerprints, 6
Fluids, 45, 46
Folic acid, 5, 43
Follicle-stimulating hormone, 2,
    3
Fraternal twins
    definition, 5
    diet of mother, 4
    in utero behavior, 150
    inheritance factors in twin-
        ning, 3–4
    occurrence, 5
Friendships, 168, 171–76

⸱G⸱

Gestational diabetes, 20
Gonadotropins, 3
Grocery store, going to, 107
    carts, 130–31
Group identity, 168

⸱H⸱

Haircutting, 60
Hand-eye coordination,
    102
Harnesses, 117
Hats, 53
Head movement, 102
Health issues, postpartum,
    123–24
Health issues, pregnancy. *See*
    Physical exercise;
    Pregnancy
Help, accepting, 65–66
High chairs, 56
Hook-on chairs, 56
Hospital stay
    bonding during, 97
    items to take, 64
Hospital tours, 62
Housework, 76, 168
Human chorionic gonadotropin,
    2
Human Genetics, 7
Human menopausal gonadotro-
    pin, 2
Hydration, 29
Hyperovulation. *See*
    Superovulation

⸱I⸱

ID bracelets, 117
Identical twins
    birthmarks, 6
    definition, 6–7

diamniotic-dichorionic
pregnancy, 6
diamniotic-monochorionic
pregnancy, 6
fingerprints, 6
in utero behavior, 150
mirror identical twins, 6–7
monoamniotic-monochorionic
pregnancy, 6
splitting of zygote, 6
Imagination, 146–47
Imitation, 146, 168
In vitro fertilization (IVT),
2–3
Incubators, 29
Independence, 176–77
Individuality, 176–77. *See also*
Twins
Infant massage, 97
Inheritance factors in twinning,
3–4, 8
Intrauterine growth restriction
(IUGR), 24
Iron, 20–21, 42–43

◦J◦

*Journal of Reproductive Medi-
cine, The,* 4

◦K◦

Kindergarten, 167–68

◦L◦

La Leche, 69
Labeling, 178
Labor drug intervention, 27, 29
Language development, 153–58.
See also Speech
Life-style changes, pregnancy,
31–47
Lungs, 16
Luteinizing hormone (LH), 3

◦M◦

Matching outfits, 53
Maternal complications,
18–22
Maternal serum alpha-
fetoprotein (MSAFP),
17–18
Maternal-fetal medicine
specialist, 13
Maternity pillows, 32, 38
Microwave ovens, 46
Milk production, 80–81
Minnesota Study of Twins
Reared Apart project,
153
Mittens, 53
Mobility, 125, 127
Monoamniotic-monochorionic
pregnancy, 6
Monozygotic twins. *See*
Identical twins
Morality, 168
Moro reflex, 73

Mother
  age, 3
  body type, 4
  diet, 4–5
  who have had previous chil-
    dren, 4
  who have had previous twins,
    4
Mothers of Twins Club, 12, 61,
  63
Motor development, 126
Multiples, statistics on,
  1–2
Muscle control, 102
Muscle tone, 101

◦ N ◦

Name brands, 61
Names
  choosing, 70
  importance of, 70
  similar-sounding, 70–71
Naps, 91, 147–49
Nature versus nurture,
  152–53
Neonatal intensive care unit
  (NICU), 13–14, 29, 96,
  150–51
  counseling, 30
Networks of help, 65–66
Night light, 115
Nighttime feedings, 87–92
Nitroglycerin, 27

Note taking, 75
Nursing, 31, 59, 74–75,
  79–86
  advantages of, 81
  mistakes, 85–86
  nighttime feeding, 90–91
  positions, 83
  supplementation, 84
Nursing pillow, 57
Nutrition, 38–39

◦ O ◦

Obstetrician, 12
  hospital affiliation, 13–14
Older children, 66–68
Onesies, 53
Ownership, 68

◦ P ◦

Pack-n-play, 55
Parenting twins
  adolescents, 181–82
  discipline, 159–60
  father's role, 98–99, 140–42
  issues of fairness, 180–81
  month 1, 73–99
  months 2–6, 101–24
  months 7–12, 125–44
  nurturing parent-child
    relations, 122–23
  school aged, 167–83

taking care of self, 76 (*See also* Spouses)
toddler years, 145–65
Pediatricians, selecting, 63
Peer pressure, 168
Perganol, 2
Perinatologist, 13
Personality development, 74, 102
Pets, 67–68
Physical exercise
　back and hip stretch, 36
　calf stretch, 35
　for pregnant women, 33–36
　side stretch, 35
　spinal curl, 34
　tailor's sit, 34
　wall push-up, 35
Phytoestrogens, 5
Pillows, 57
　Boppy, 57
　nursing, 57
Pincer grasp, 126
Placenta, 6, 8
Placenta previa, 21
Plastic bathtub, 55
Play, 95. *See also* Toys
　games, 137–38
　parallel play, 125, 151
Play groups, 113
Playpen, 55
Podcasts, 115
Port-a-crib, 55
Postpartum depression, 77–79
Preeclampsia, 20

Pregnancy
　abruptio placenta, 21
　anemia, 20–21
　bleeding, 19
　bonding during, 97
　cesarean sections, 12, 21–22
　choosing a doctor, 12–13
　comfort, 37–38
　diet, 38–46
　edema, 19
　gestational diabetes, 20
　interventions to prolong, 26–29
　life-style changes, 31–47
　placenta previa, 21
　preeclampsia, 20
　prenatal care, 12
　risks, 11–12, 14
　sexual relations, 36–37
　tests, 14–18
　tips, 46–47
　traveling, 38
　working, 37
Pregnyl, 2
Premature babies, 29–31
　"adjusted age," 74
　bathing, 93
　bonding with, 30–31, 96
　dressing, 93
　twin bonding, 150–51
Prenatal care, 46
Prenatal tests
　amniocentesis, 15–16
　chorionic villus sampling (CVS), 16–17

maternal serum alpha-
fetoprotein (MSAFP),
17–18
nonstress test (NST), 18
ultrasound, 14–15
Preterm labor, 24–29
drug intervention, 27, 29
interventions to prolong
pregnancy, 26–29
warning signs, 25–26
Private language, 146
Protein, 41–42
Public attention, 108–9
Pulling up, 126
Pushing the envelope,
146

•R•

Race factors in twinning,
4
Radiation, 46
Respiratory distress syndrome
(RDS), 29
Respiratory problems, 29
Rocking chairs, 59
Rolling (mobility), 125
Rooting reflex, 73
Routines
bedtime, 91
putting babies on a schedule,
110–13
Rules of behavior, 128

•S•

Safety issues, 130–31
babyproofing, 103, 128–30
rules of behavior, 128
Salt, 43
Scent, 31
Schedules. *See* Routines
School issues
same classroom, 168–73
Self-control, 147
Self-esteem, 168
Semi-identical twins, 5, 7
Sense of humor, 102
Sex determination, 16
Sexual relations, 36–37
Sibling bonds, 68, 121–22
Sickle-cell anemia, 16
Sickness, 164
Sign language, 155
Singing, 74, 102, 155
Single embryo transfer (SET), 3
Sitting up, 125
Sleeping, 46, 74, 76
preparing two babies at once,
105–6
tips for pregnant women, 32,
33
Sling, 57
Smoking, 45, 46
Snugly sack, 55
Speech, 103
babbling, 146
commands, 146
development of, 153–58

difficulties in twins, 155–56
first words, 154
private language, 146, 156
understanding, 126
Spina bifida, 17
Spontaneous abortion, 17
Spouses, 70, 118
keeping marriage on track,
139–41
marital intimacy, 119
Steinman, Gary, 4–5
Stretch suits, 53
Strollers, 51–52, 56, 57
umbrella, 117–18
Sucking, 73
Sudden infant death syndrome
(SIDS), 45
Sulfate IV, 27
Sunlight, 5
Superovulation, 1, 5
Superyard, 127
Support groups, 113
Support hose, 38
Swings, 52
Synthetic growth hormones, 4–5

°T°

Talking to babies, 154–55
Tay-Sachs disease, 16, 17
Telegraphic phrase, 154
Telephone habits, 76. *See also*
Finances
Terrible twos, 158–64
Thank-you notes, 69
Toilet training, 162–64
Touching, 31, 74
Toys, 52, 61, 95, 115
Transitional objects, 92
Travel strollers, 56
Traveling
car travel, 114, 130
equipment, 114–15, 117–18
getting out of the house,
106–8
overnight, 114–18
by plane, 116–17
seat assignments, 107–8
T-shirts, 53
Twin clubs, 69
Twin language, 146, 156
Twin Research, 3
Twin types. *See also* Fraternal
twins; Identical twins; Semi-
identical twins
determining, 7–8
Twins. *See also specific topics*
adolescents, 181–82
adults, 182
comparing and contrasting,
177–78
competition between, 179
fighting between, 160–62
individual attention, 112–13
individual persons, 131–34,
176–78
month 1, 73–99

months 2–6, 101–24
months 7–12, 125–44
myths, 8
personality differences, 74,
    102
risks in pregnancy, 11–12,
    14
school aged, 167–83
separating for a day, 134–36
statistics, 1–2
telling apart, 76–77
toddler years, 145–65
Twin-to-twin transfusion syn-
    drome (TTTS), 15, 23–24

◦U◦

Ultrasound, 7–8, 14–15
Umbilical cord, blood testing of,
    7
Umbrella strollers, 56

◦V◦

Vaginal births, 12
Vibrating bouncer seats, 49, 50,
    92
Vitamin supplements, 43
Vocalization, 102

◦W◦

Walking, 126
Weight. *See* Birth weight
Weight gain in pregnancy, 11
    tips, 43–45
Weight loss after pregnancy,
    123–24
Working, 37

◦Y◦

Yams, 5